The
WISDOM
of
THE TAO

OTHER TITLES IN THIS SERIES

The Wisdom of Hinduism, ISBN 1–85168–227–9

The Wisdom of Jesus, ISBN 1–85168–225–2

The Wisdom of Buddhism, ISBN 1–85168–226–0

The Wisdom of the Qur'an, ISBN 1–85168–224–4

The Wisdom of Judaism, ISBN 1–85168–228–7

RELATED TITLES PUBLISHED BY ONEWORLD

God's BIG Book of Virtues

God's BIG Handbook for the Soul

God's BIG Instruction Book

The Oneworld Book of Prayer

Words to Comfort, Words to Heal

The
WISDOM
of
THE TAO

Compiled and edited by Julian F. Pas

ONEWORLD

OXFORD

THE WISDOM OF THE TAO

Oneworld Publications
(Sales and Editorial)
185 Banbury Road
Oxford OX2 7AR
England
http://www.oneworld-publications.com

Oneworld Publications
(US Marketing Office)
160 N Washington St.
4th Floor, Boston
MA 02114
USA

ISBN 1–85168–232–5

Cover and text design by Design Deluxe, Bath
Printed by Graphicom Srl, Vicenza, Italy

CONTENTS

All photographs reproduced in this volume
were taken by the editor.

PREFACE

TAOISM IS one of the major cultural traditions dating back to ancient China. It includes a philosophical–mystical stream, whose major texts are the *Daodejing* and the *Zhuangzi* dating from the fourth and third centuries BCE; and a purely religious system with priesthood and scriptures, which originated in the second century CE, and is still being practised in China today.

Although of different origins, the two streams have been combined in later history and appear as one body in the minds of many Taoist practitioners.

In the present collection I have selected a variety of texts from both streams, with an emphasis on the mystical aspects of the tradition that ring a familiar chord in our Western minds. Taoism, indeed, has a universal appeal revealing a richness of ideas and practices comparable to an oriental rock garden where trees, flowers, rocks and streams evoke a sense of profound mystery and oneness with nature. The Taoist texts selected here evoke a similar sense of mystery: like oriental gardens they exemplify the oneness of nature and humanity, the integration of the natural world and human aspiration, or to use a more common expression, the unity of nature and culture.

These Taoist texts do not evoke a sense of religious worship. Although the later scriptures of the Taoist religion are products of a strictly religious worldview, the earlier philosophical texts are different: they are rather humanistic in scope, although they also suggest a feeling of transcendence, but a transcendence of the Tao, not a deity, as a kind of ultimate, all-encompassing reality.

Reading the Taoist wisdom texts is like wandering through our mystery rock garden. The variety of ideas one encounters resembles the infinite variety of flowers and plants spread around rocks and ponds: both inspire in us a sense of mystery and of oneness with a transcendent reality.

Most of the texts are ancient and derive from a cultural setting very different from our own, so it is a surprise to find in them themes and ideas very dear and familiar to us in the West of the twenty-first century. It is recommended that the texts be read and reread, leading one to continuously discover new meanings in them, thus widening and deepening our own spiritual horizon. To grow in wisdom is a process of steady and ongoing transformation.

At this point, I'd like to say a word of thanks to a few persons who helped me to complete this little volume. My wife Yü-lin was very supportive of this project and in particular aided with the translation of some Chinese texts. My daughter

Sonya proofread and skilfully copy-edited the complete text, whereas my colleague and friend Scott Dunbar was helpful in reviewing part of the first draft. Sonya, as well as Audry Swan, were excellent in word-processing the whole manuscript. Further, I am most grateful to Paul Crowe for providing the Chinese characters to illustrate the texts. Finally, I appreciate the encouragement and assistance provided by the publisher.

JANUARY 2000

❊ ❊ ❊

A practical note on the word 'Taoism'. The etymology indicates a combination of the Chinese term (or 'character') Tao, with the English ending '-ism'. Tao here means the 'Way', and will be explored in later texts. The same word also means 'road, path', even 'street' in ordinary language. In 'Taoism', however, Tao has been transformed into a 'Way' of life, a particular Chinese vision of reality. Taoism, together with Confucianism and (Chinese) Buddhism comprise what we call the three 'Teachings' of China: three schools of thought that also have religious dimensions (especially in the cases of Taoism and Buddhism).

These preliminaries should be sufficient to start us on the 'Way'. I wish you a happy journey through the mystery garden of Taoist wisdom.

A NOTE ABOUT TRANSLITERATION

CHINESE IS a non-alphabetical language, but to make characters intelligible to Western readers, systems of transliteration have been devised so that Chinese characters can be written with the use of our alphabet.

Currently, the two most popular systems are the Wade–Giles system (named after its authors) and the *pinyin* system, introduced by the People's Republic of China in recent times. Whereas the Wade–Giles system is still used by the Library of Congress and many academics, the *pinyin* system is used in newscasting and in a growing number of academic writings.

In this little volume I use the *pinyin* system: it is more convenient and consistent. I even change Wade–Giles spellings in quotations of published works for the sake of clarity and consistency.

The only exceptions are the words 'Tao', 'Taoism', and 'Taoist' (which would be 'Dao', 'Daoism', and 'Daoist' when expressed in *pinyin*): these were already words adopted into the English language before the People's Republic came into existence, and I prefer to use them as English terms rather than changing them back to romanized Chinese.

THE SCRIPTURES OF TAOISM

SINCE TAOISM is just beginning to be known in the West, it is important briefly to introduce its basic scriptures, on which the tradition is based.

The two streams mentioned in the Preface each have their own scriptures: the philosophical–mystical stream's major writings are the *Guanzi*, the *Daodejing*, the *Zhuangzi*, the *Liezi* and the *Huainanzi*.

The religious stream's scriptures are all found in the Taoist Canon (which also includes the scriptures of the former stream). It is a collection of over 1480 texts, compiled and edited in 1444–5, during the Ming dynasty.

This great quantity of texts was produced over many centuries by different schools of Taoism, and reflects the many interests and methods of Taoist practitioners. Some scriptures deal with meditation and spiritual cultivation, others are manuals of Taoist liturgy; still others have a predominantly ethical concern. Some are purely historical records. Together they are an important collection of writings, not only for specifically Taoist history and practice, but also for our understanding of Chinese culture and literature as a whole.

Since I shall heavily quote selections of the philosophical–mystical tradition, I feel it is crucial to give a short description of each of these texts. The quotations from the religious writings of the Taoist Canon are fewer: each text quoted will be briefly introduced.

THE *DAODEJING*   Also known as the *Laozi*, this was probably written by various 'old sages' around 300 to 250 BCE. It is addressed to rulers of the country, urging them not only to be competent administrators, but also to dedicate themselves to the contemplation of the Tao and to spiritual self-cultivation. Only a ruler who combines political acumen with a deep insight into the nature and operations of the Tao can lead his people to well-being and contentment. That means that the best leader of men is someone who interferes the least in the lives of the people. This idea is expressed in the concept of *wuwei* (literally translated 'non-action'), which can be called the quintessence of Taoist rulership.

This short text (5000 characters in Chinese), is very popular both in China and beyond. Over 250 translations exist in Western languages. And the love affair is not over yet: new translations still appear at irregular intervals.

In the 1970s two new versions of the *Daodejing* were excavated from an ancient tomb in China's Hunan province. They are called the 'silk manuscripts' (of Mawangdui, near Changsha) and date from about 200 BCE. They are at least 400 years older than the transmitted text previously known to us. Yet despite the 400-year difference, the silk manuscripts are very similar to the transmitted text. The major difference is the reversal of the two parts of the booklet: instead of discussing *Tao* and *Te*, they discourse on *Te* and *Tao*.

The *Daodejing* today is still a source of inspiration for those who strive for spiritual perfection without being tied down by religious dogma. It is a manifest of humanistic spiritual culture and enrichment.

THE *GUANZI*   A large syncretist collection dating from the fourth century BCE, this contains two Taoist-oriented essays titled *Neiye* ('Inward Training') and *Xinshu* ('Techniques of the Mind'). It is concerned with inner transformation leading to the attainment of mystical union and understanding. The *Guanzi* is little known but is an important document connected with the very beginning of the Taoist worldview.

THE *ZHUANGZI*   This consists of thirty-three chapters, seven of which are called 'Inner Chapters' and are believed to have been written by a fourth-century-BCE thinker named Zhuang Zhou or Zhuangzi (Master Zhuang). The later chapters ('Outer' and 'Miscellaneous') were written in various periods, from the third to the second century BCE. As can be expected, the multiple authorship explains the presence of different tendencies in the text, which are not always in agreement with the original message of the Inner Chapters.

The *Zhuangzi* is a very important literary and philosophical document, full of fascinating anecdotes and analogies, and allows us to intuit Zhuangzi's personality as a great sage looking at the world of men with irony and humour. The Inner Chapters are an expression of his experience of transcendence: wandering in mystical flight beyond the mediocre world of society is his ultimate wish and destination.

THE *LIEZI*   A small volume of essays, attributed to a person named Liezi (Master Lie), who often appears in Taoist texts as a sage, but whose historicity remains doubtful. However, the text exists and dates from perhaps 300 CE, although many parts, such as several stories that also appear in the *Zhuangzi*, are certainly older.

In style, the *Liezi* is similar to the *Zhuangzi*: it contains anecdotes, discussions and dialogues reminiscent of its prototype. Through them we become aware of some important views of the author. They illustrate, as A. C. Graham states, that the Taoism of the *Liezi* 'coincides with the scientific world view [of today]: . . . the littleness of man in a vast universe; . . . the transience of life, the impossibility of knowing what comes after death, . . .' (Graham: 12–13).

THE *HUAINANZI* A collection of twenty-one essays, edited in the second century BCE (c. 139 BCE) by the Prince of Huainan, Liu An. Aspiring to the imperial throne but frustrated in his efforts, Liu An applied his energy to the study of contemporary knowledge. In his court, he gathered a large number of scholars whom he supported and encouraged in advanced studies and writing. The *Huainanzi* is the collection of essays produced by the joint efforts of these court scholars. Several, though not all of them, are of Taoist inspiration.

Today the *Huainanzi* has become a favourite subject in sinology, as it offers a gold mine of information about the intellectual climate of the Han period and even the period leading up to it.

THE MYSTERY OF THE
TAO AND ITS POWER

TAO: SUPREME REALITY BEYOND WORDS

The Word Tao (Way), is just a convenient term used to name something that is essentially unnameable and beyond the power of language. Although it is also immanent in all beings, it cannot be grasped.

THE WAY that can be expressed in words is not the
    everlasting Way.
Names by which it is named are not everlasting
    names.

Daodejing 1

THE WAY cannot be thought of as being, nor can it be thought of as non-being. In calling it the Way we are only adopting a temporary expedient . . .
The Perfection of the Way and things – neither words nor silence are worthy of expressing it. Not to talk, nor to be silent – this is the highest form of debate.

Zhuangzi 25

THE WAY has its reality and its signs but is without action or form. You can hand it down but you cannot receive it; you can get it but you cannot see it. It is its own source, its own root. Before Heaven and earth existed it was there, firm from ancient times. It gave spirituality to the spirits and to [the ancestral *Di*]; it gave birth to Heaven and earth. It exists beyond the highest point, and yet you cannot call it lofty; it exists beneath the limit of the six directions and yet you cannot call it deep. It was born before Heaven and earth, and yet you cannot say it has been there for long; it is earlier than the earliest time, and yet you cannot call it old.

Zhuangzi 6: 'The Great and Venerable Teacher'; Watson: 81

ONE STARES at it but does not see it:
    it is called 'colourless'.
One listens to it but does not hear it:
    it is called 'soundless'.
One grasps it but does not hold it:
    it is called 'formless'.
These three cannot be fathomed any deeper,
    indeed, they converge into oneness.

Daodejing 14

THE TAO is nameless wholeness.

Daodejing 32

TAO: THE CREATIVE

The Tao is impersonal transcendent reality, out of which all existence arises. It is a process of continuous creativity and transformation, identical with Cosmic Reality, yet more sublime in essence.

> THE TAO generated the One.
> The One generated the Two.
> The Two generated the Three.
> The Three generated all beings.
> All beings carry yin on their back and hold yang in
>   their arms.
> When their energies clash, harmony ensues.

Daodejing 42

HOW POWERFUL flows the Tao,
   Meandering left and right!
All beings rely on it for existence
   And it does not reject them.
It accomplishes its task, but does not glorify in it.

Daodejing 34

THERE WAS something formed out of chaos,
   Which existed before heaven-and-earth.
How solitary! How still!
   It exists on its own without inner change.
It circulates everywhere without creating danger.
   It can be considered the mother of under-heaven.
I do not know its name: I call it 'Tao'.

Daodejing 25

THAT 'THING' Tao is really vague, really elusive.
How vague! How elusive! Yet in it are 'forms'.
How vague! How elusive! Yet in it are 'things'.
How obscure! How mysterious! Yet in it are 'seeds of
   life'.
These seeds are real, in them there is 'trust'.

Daodejing 21

THE TAO generates them [the myriad living beings],
   Its power sustains them.
   Material things give them shape.
   Circumstances complete them.
Therefore:
   Of all beings none does not honour the Tao
   Nor value its power.
To honour the Tao and valuate its power,
   There is no command: it happens of its own accord.

The Tao generates them
   Makes them grow,
   Feeds them,
   Shelters and regulates them,
   Nourishes and protects them.
It generates but does not possess.
It acts but does not grasp.
It leads but does not dominate.
This is called mysterious power.

Daodejing 51

DARK AND hidden, [the Way] seems not to exist and yet it is there; lush and unbounded, it possesses no form but only spirit; the ten thousand things are shepherded by it, though they do not understand it – this is what is called the Source, the Root.

Zhuangzi 22: 'Knowledge Wandered North'; Watson: 237

HOW THE TAO OPERATES

The Tao operates in a paradoxical manner: it seems not to do anything, yet everything is accomplished. It does all things without effort, in weakness. It repeats its actions continuously, as if in never-ending circles.

Though bright, it appears dark; though it appears weak, it is strong and irresistible.

Only a sage-ruler who emulates the Tao is able to benefit all living beings.

THE TAO is great . . .
  It is its own model.

Daodejing 25

THE TAO constantly does not 'act'
  But there is nothing it does not do.

Daodejing 37

REVERSAL (REPETITION) is the movement of Tao.
Weakness is the method of Tao.

Daodejing 40

THE BRIGHT Tao is like darkness.
The progressive Tao is like going backwards.
The even Tao is like rough.

Daodejing 41

TAO IS empty
　　But in its functioning
　　There is nothing it does not fill.

Daodejing 4

WHAT IS contrary to the Tao
　　Comes to an early end.

Daodejing 30; 55

WHEN THE Tao 'speaks',
　　How bland! It has no flavour.
Look at it: it is not worth seeing.
Listen to it: it is not worth hearing.
Use it, however: it is inexhaustible.

Daodejing 35

THE TAO is the storehouse of all beings,
　　The treasure of the good people
　　And [even] the protection of the not-good people.

Daodejing 62

WHO IS able to have abundance to present to all in the
　　land?
Only he/she who has the Tao.

Daodejing 77

SYMBOLS OF THE TAO

Since we are unable to 'grasp' the essence of Tao through rational language and rational thinking, symbols allow us to gain an intuitive insight into its mystery. Rich in imaginative power, these symbols stir our intuitive imagination. In the Daodejing, the most common symbols are water, the feminine, the valley, the infant, and uncarved wood.

Water is essential to all that lives and yet does not demand recognition. It is humble. In its weakness it is strong. Water is also a symbol of the mind's stillness.

HIGHEST GOODNESS is like water.
The goodness of water is to benefit all beings without
    competing.
It sinks down to places which everyone dislikes.
Therefore it is close to the Tao.

Daodejing 8

NOTHING UNDER heaven is softer and more pliable than
    water;
But in attacking the hard and rigid nothing is more
    effective.

Daodejing 78

MEN DO not mirror themselves in running water –
    they mirror themselves in still water.
Only what is still can still the stillness of all things.

Zhuangzi 5

The feminine or female, also called the mother, is a symbol of the Tao in a twofold way. First, in the view of the Taoist authors, woman is considered to be humble, modest, weak, yet through weakness she overcomes the man's power. Secondly, identified with the Tao, the mother generates new life, and with motherly care, fosters and protects this new life.

THE NAMELESS [Tao] is the beginning of heaven-and-earth.
The nameable [Tao] is the mother of all beings.

Daodejing 1

THE WORLD has a beginning,
   It may be considered the mother of the world.
Once one knows the mother,
   Through her one knows her children.
Once one knows her children,
   Then returns and holds on to the mother,
   He will not be in danger throughout his life.

Daodejing 52

A GREAT state is like the lower reaches of a river,
   The merging point of all streams under heaven,
   The female under heaven.
The female constantly overcomes the male through stillness.
   In stillness she is below [the male].

Daodejing 61

The valley resembles the symbolism of the feminine: it suggests humility (it lies low in contrast with hills and mountains) as well as fertility: water flows to it and it becomes the origin of new life.

THE VALLEY spirit does not die:
    It is called the mysterious feminine.
The gate of entry to the mysterious feminine
    Is called the root of heaven-and-earth.

Daodejing 6

WHO KNOWS glory but holds on to disgrace
    Is like a valley in the land.
Who is a valley in the land
    His/her constant power is abundant.
    He/she returns to wholeness (*pu*).

Daodejing 28

The infant is another symbol of the Tao. It is weak and totally depends on its mother for survival and growth. In the newly born infant, the vital energy or qi with which all living beings are born, is complete and intact. It possesses the fullness of the Tao. Being unselfconscious, the infant is innocent and does not calculate, thus wild animals do not feel threatened and will not harm it.

ONE WHO possesses abundant power (*de*)
    May be compared to a newborn baby.
Poisonous insects or poisonous snakes do not sting it.
Wild beasts do not seize it.
Birds of prey do not attack it.
Its bones are soft, its tendons flexible.
    But its grasp is firm.
It does not know sexual union yet, but its organ is
    erect:
It is the apex of its essence.

Daodejing 55

Uncarved wood (pu), which occurs almost unnoticed in the Daodejing, refers to wood that has not yet been carved into objects (utensils, furniture, etc.). In its original condition, it is a symbol of the Tao as being untouched, untainted, undivided, in its state of primordial wholeness.

THE TAO is nameless wholeness (*pu*) . . .
When one starts to divide, names arise.

Daodejing 32

THE EXCELLENT gentlemen of old
   Were sublime and had deep insight,
Too profound to understand. . . .
Careful, as when one crosses a river in winter.
Timid, as if one expects danger from all sides.
Flexible, like ice about to melt.
Authentic, like uncarved wood.

Daodejing 15

I GIVE the people this concrete advice:
  Show authenticity, hold on to wholeness (*pu*)
  Lower selfishness, reduce desires.

Daodejing 19

THE POWER OF THE TAO

The Tao's power, De (also spelled Te), is an elusive concept. It is often translated as 'virtue', but this tends to give the wrong impression. De refers to the inherent nature of all beings, as instilled in them by the Tao. It is their inherent potential for action in accordance with their own individual nature.

In the ruler, De is also charisma, like magic power emanating from his inner self, cultivated by stillness and contemplation. It includes deep knowledge, wisdom, even moral virtues such as goodness, frugality, sincerity, integrity. A good leader, who has Te/De, nourishes his people without self-seeking; he acts, like the Tao, 'without action'.

TO GENERATE and nourish,
To generate and not to possess,
To act and not to grasp.
To lead and not to dominate:
This is called 'mysterious power'.

Daodejing 10

THE MANIFESTATIONS of great power
    emanate from the Tao alone.

Daodejing 21

WHOEVER IS a ravine in the land
    Does not lose his/her constant power
    And returns to infancy.

Daodejing 28

SUPERIOR POWER is not power,
    Therefore it has power.
Inferior power does not give up its power,
    Therefore it has no power.
Superior power does not act,
    And has no motive to act.
Inferior power acts,
    And has a motive to act.

Daodejing 38

SUPERIOR POWER is like a valley . . .
Extensive power appears insufficient.
Solid power appears exhausted.

Daodejing 41

CULTIVATE THE Tao in your own person:
  Your power will be authentic.
Cultivate the Tao in your family:
  Its power will be plentiful.
Cultivate the Tao in your community:
  Its power will last.
Cultivate the Tao in the country:
  Its power will be abundant.
Cultivate the Tao in the world:
  Its power will be pervasive.

Daodejing 54

ONE WHO possesses abundant power
    May be compared to a newborn baby.

Daodejing 55

ALWAYS TO know the correct standard
    Is called mysterious power.
Mysterious power is deep and far-reaching.

Daodejing 65

THE TAO IS EVERYWHERE

The Tao is an omnipresent reality. Since it originates all beings, they all share some of its nature. High and low, the Tao is in all things.

MASTER DONGGUO asked Zhuangzi, 'This thing called the Way – where does it exist?'
Zhuangzi said, 'There is no place it doesn't exist.'
'Come,' said Master Dongguo, 'you must be more specific!'
'It is in the ant.'
'As low a thing as that?'
'It is in the panic grass.'
'But that's lower still!'
'It is in the tiles and shards.'
'How can it be so low?'
'It is in the piss and shit.'
Master Dongguo made no reply.

Zhuangzi 22: 'Knowledge Wandered North'; Watson: 240–1

CAN ONE POSSESS THE TAO?

SHUN ASKED Cheng, 'Is it possible to gain possession of the Way?'

'You don't even have possession of your own body – how could you possibly gain possession of the Way?'

'If I don't have possession of my own body, then who does?' said Shun.

'It is a form lent you by Heaven and earth. You do not have possession of life – it is a harmony lent by Heaven and earth. You do not have possession of your inborn nature and fate – they are contingencies lent by Heaven and earth. You do not have possession of your sons and grandsons – they are castoff skins lent by Heaven and earth.' . . .

'How could it be possible to gain possession of anything?'

Zhuangzi 22: 'Knowledge Wandered North'; Watson: 238

COSMIC REALITY,
LIFE AND DEATH

HEAVEN-AND-EARTH: COSMIC REALITY

What we today call the 'cosmos' was expressed by 'heaven-and-earth' in ancient China. It is almost synonymous with our modern concept of 'nature', which is the visible expression of the Tao, or the Tao that 'can be talked about'.

This 'heaven-and-earth' has its own existence, independent from human beings and other creatures. Although it provides all that is needed for the birth and growth of those beings, it does not really do so on purpose nor does it care for them. It is impartial, to the point of indifference.

WHEN HEAVEN and Earth were yet unformed,
All was ascending and flying, diving and delving.
Thus it was called the Great Inception.
The [Tao] began in the Nebulous Void.
The Nebulous Void produced space–time;
Space–time produced the primordial qi.
A shoreline (divided) the primordial qi.
That which was pure and bright spread out to form Heaven;
The heavy and turbid congealed to form Earth.

Huainanzi, Book Three: 'Treatise on the Patterns of
Heaven'; trans. Major: 62

HEAVEN-AND-Earth are not benevolent:
It treats all beings as straw-dogs.

Daodejing 5

During a banquet, Tian of Qi said to his guests:

'HOW GENEROUS heaven is to mankind! It grows the five grains and breeds the fish and birds for the use of man.'

All the guests answered like his echo. But a twelve-year-old boy of the Pao family, who had a seat among the guests, came forward and said:

'It is not as your lordship says. The myriad things between heaven and earth, born in the same way that we are, do not differ from us in kind. One kind is no nobler than another; it is simply that the stronger and cleverer rule the weaker and sillier. Things take it in turns to eat each other, but they are not bred for each other's sake. Men take the things which are edible and eat them, but how can it be claimed that heaven bred them originally for the sake of man? Besides, mosquitoes and gnats bite our skin, tigers and wolves eat our flesh; did heaven originally breed man for the sake of mosquitoes and gnats, and his flesh for the sake of tigers and wolves?'

Liezi 8: 'Explaining Conjunctions'; Graham: 178–9

There is, however, a balance in nature, which is fair to all; it is unlike human action.

> THE WAY of heaven is to reduce the excessive
>   And to increase the insufficient.
> The human way is not like it: it reduces
>   the insufficient to present it to the excessive.

Daodejing 77

> THE WAY of heaven is to be without favouritism,
>   But it constantly assists the good people.

Daodejing 79

> THE WAY of heaven is to benefit, not to harm.
> The way of the sage is to act, but not to compete.

Daodejing 81

THE WAY of heaven is not to compete, yet is good at
  gaining victory;
It does not speak, yet is good at being responsive;
It does not summon, yet things come of their own
  accord;
Unhurried, it is good at planning.
Heaven's net is all-embracing:
  Its meshes are wide, but nothing escapes.

Daodejing 73

*The role of humanity is to co-operate with the potentialities of
heaven-and-earth (nature) to reach its destiny. Alone, none of
the 'actors' is able to achieve anything.*

HEAVEN AND earth cannot achieve everything;
The sage is not capable of everything;
None of the myriad things can be used for
  everything.
For this reason
  It is the office of heaven to beget and to shelter,
  The office of earth to shape and to support,
  The office of the sage to teach and to reform,
  The office of each thing to perform its function.

Liezi 1: 'Heaven's Gifts'; Graham: 19

Heaven and Earth: Cosmic Reality ↜ 49

Will this cosmos in which we live come to an end? Opinions among the Taoists are divided; most likely we have no way to know. Here is one man's view:

HEAVEN AND earth are one tiny thing within the void, the largest among things that exist. It is no doubt true that it will be long before they reach their term and come to an end, and that it is no easy matter to estimate and predict when this will happen. To worry about them perishing is indeed wide of the mark; but to say they will never perish is also open to objection. Since heaven and earth are bound to perish, a time will come when they will perish.

Liezi 1: 'Heaven's Gifts'; Graham: 28–9

On the other hand, Liezi does not argue. Smiling, he says:

IT IS nonsense to say either that heaven and earth will perish or that they will not. Whether they will perish or not we can never know. . . .
Why should we care whether they perish or not?

Liezi 1: 'Heaven's Gifts'; Graham: 29

This Taoist view is similar to what the Buddha thought: among the four things that he refused to discuss was the question of whether the world is eternal or not. It is impossible to know and, moreover, irrelevant.

THE HEAVENLY AND THE HUMAN

The 'heavenly' is that which is given by nature; the 'human' is man-made, that which is added to what is naturally given, often contrary to basic human nature. This theme is found in the Daodejing, *but is more strongly emphasized in the* Zhuangzi.

If human efforts go against inborn nature, the true Way is being lost; if the heavenly and the human are in harmony, the Way prevails and good things happen: the world is at peace. Yet the 'facts of life' are that humans interfere too much with what is from heaven, and thus spoil the state of things: this is chaos.

I T IS said: the Heavenly is on the inside, the human is on the outside. Virtue resides in the Heavenly. Understand the actions of Heaven and man, base yourself upon Heaven, take your stand in virtue, and then, although you hasten or hold back, bend or stretch, you may return to the essential and speak of the ultimate.

'What do you mean by the Heavenly and the human?'

Ro of the North Sea said, 'Horses and oxen have four feet – this is what I mean by the Heavenly. Putting a halter on the horse's head, piercing the ox's nose – this is what I mean by the human. So I say: do not let what is human wipe out what is

Heavenly; do not let what is purposeful wipe out what is fated; do not let [the desire for] gain lead you after fame. Be cautious, guard it, and do not lose it – this is what I mean by returning to the True.'

Zhuangzi 17: 'Autumn Floods'; Watson, 182–3

The 'perfect man', in the Zhuangzi, cultivates in himself what is of heaven and shuns what is artificial or man-made.

HE WHO knows what it is that Heaven does, and knows what it is that man does, has reached the peak. Knowing what it is that Heaven does, he lives with Heaven. Knowing what it is that man does, he uses the knowledge of what he knows to help out the knowledge of what he doesn't know, and lives out the years that Heaven gave him without being cut off midway. This is the perfection of knowledge.

Zhuangzi 6: 'The Great and Venerable Teacher'; Watson: 77

To know, however, what is of heaven, and what is not, is a difficult task.

HOW CAN I know that what I call Heaven is not really man, and what I call man is not really Heaven?

> *Zhuangzi 6:* 'The Great and Venerable Teacher';
> Watson: 77

What human society often does to nature is to force it into actions or functions not compatible with nature. It can only lead to disaster.

HAVEN'T YOU heard this story? Once a sea bird alighted in the suburbs of the Lu capital. The marquis of Lu escorted it to the ancestral temple, where he entertained it, performing music . . . for it to listen to and presenting it with the meat of the . . . sacrifice to feast on. But the bird only looked dazed and forlorn, refusing to eat a single slice of meat or drink a cup of wine, and in three days it was dead.

> *Zhuangzi 18:* 'Perfect Happiness'; Watson: 194

D O NOT try [therefore] to develop what is natural to man; develop what is natural to Heaven. He who develops Heaven benefits life; he who develops man injures life.

Zhuangzi 19: 'Mastering Life'; Watson: 199

W HEN A drunken man falls from a carriage, though the carriage may be going very fast, he won't be killed. He has bones and joints the same as other men, and yet he is not injured as they would be, because his spirit is whole. He didn't know he was riding, and he doesn't know he has fallen out. Life and death, alarm and terror do not enter his breast, . . . If he can keep himself whole like this by means of wine, how much more can he keep himself whole by means of Heaven! The sage hides himself in Heaven – hence there is nothing that can do him harm.

Zhuangzi 19: 'Mastering Life'; Watson: 198–9

DESTINY AND HUMAN EFFORT

One of the most intriguing problems in life is the role of free will versus fate. Where the dividing line lies between the 'decree of heaven' (fate) and 'human action' (free will) is a central problem in Chinese philosophy.

Confucius holds that long life and wealth are decided by fate, but still human action should be determined by ethical principles. The Taoist master Liezi claims that all our efforts are powerless against destiny. This is extreme fatalism, not shared by all Taoists.

In the first text, Destiny addresses Effort, and discusses their relative influences on human events.

'IF [SUCCESS and life duration are] within the reach of your endeavour, why did you give long life to one and early death to the other, why did you permit the sage to fail and villains to succeed, demean an able man and exalt a fool, impoverish good men and enrich a bad one?'

'If it is as you say, [effort responds] certainly I have no effect on things. But is it you who directs that things should be so?' . . .

'Long life and short, [destiny answers] failure and success, high rank and low, wealth and poverty, come about of themselves. What can I know about it? What can I know about it?'

Liezi 6: 'Endeavor and Destiny'; Graham: 121–2

To LIVE and die at the right time is a blessing from heaven. Not to live when it is time to live, not to die when it is time to die, is a punishment from heaven. Some get life and death at the right times, some live and die when it is not time to live and die. But it is neither other things nor ourselves that give us life when we live and death when we die; both are destined, wisdom can do nothing about them.

Liezi 6: 'Endeavor and Destiny'; Graham: 127

SOME VALUE life and live, some scorn it and die, some take care of the body and do it good, some neglect it and do it harm. This seems only reasonable but it is not; in these cases also life and death, good and harm, come of themselves.

Liezi 6: 'Endeavor and Destiny'; Graham 129

FARMERS HURRY to keep up with the seasons, merchants run after profit, craftsmen chase new skills, officials hunt power; the pressure of their circumstances makes this so. But farmers meet with both water and drought, merchants with both gain and loss, craftsmen with both success and failure, officials with both good luck and ill; destiny makes this so.

Liezi 6: 'Endeavor and Destiny'; Graham 133–4

IN THE world, there are two great decrees: one is fate and the other is duty. That a son should love his parents is fate – you cannot erase this from his heart. That a subject should serve his ruler is duty – there is no place he can go and be without his ruler, no place he can escape to between heaven and earth. These are called the great decrees. Therefore, to serve your parents and be content to follow them anywhere – this is the perfection of filial piety. To serve your ruler and be content to do anything for him – this is the peak of loyalty. And to serve your own mind so that sadness or joy do not sway or move it; to understand what you can do nothing about and to be content with it as with fate – this is the perfection of virtue.

Zhuangzi 4: 'In the World of Men'; Watson: 59–60

LIFE AND DEATH ARE FATED

This topic closely follows the one of destiny and human effort. The most striking example is narrated in the Zhuangzi: after Zhuangzi's wife had died, his friend Huizi went to offer his condolences, but found Zhuangzi pounding on a tub and singing. Huizi, scandalized, remonstrates with him. Zhuangzi, in turn, tells his friend that he does not understand anything about fate.

WHEN SHE first died, do you think I didn't grieve like anyone else? But I looked back to her beginning and the time before she was born. Not only the time before she was born, but the time before she had a body. Not only the time before she had a body, but the time before she had a spirit [*qi*]. In the midst of the jumble of wonder and mystery a change took place and she had a spirit. Another change and she had a body. Another change and she was born. Now there's been another change and she is dead. It's just like the progression of the four seasons, spring, summer, fall, winter.

Now she's going to lie peacefully in a vast room. If I were to follow after her bawling and sobbing, it would show that I don't understand anything about fate.

Zhuangzi 18: 'Perfect Happiness'; Watson: 192

LIFE AND death are fated – constant as the succession of dark and dawn, a matter of Heaven. There are some things which man can do nothing about – all are a matter of the nature of [things].

Zhuangzi 6: 'The Great and Venerable Teacher'; Watson: 80

If life and death are fated, it does not make sense to grieve over the passing away of dear ones.

THERE WAS a man of Wei, . . . who did not grieve when his son died. His wife said to him: 'Not one in the world loved his son as much as you did. Why do you not grieve now he is dead?'

'I used to have no son,' he answered, 'and when I had no son I did not grieve. Now that he is dead, it is the same as it was before when I had no son. Why should I grieve over him?'

Liezi 6: 'Endeavor and Destiny'; Graham: 133

ACCEPTING DEATH IS WISDOM

If life and death are fated, there is not much we can do about it. Efforts to reach immortality are futile. The only sensible attitude is to accept death as a positive value. Only thus can we begin to live, or to enjoy living. The Taoist sage is such a person: he/she accepts both life and death as equally good: this is submitting to fate with a smile.

THE TRUE Man of ancient times knew nothing of loving life, knew nothing of hating death. He emerged without delight; he went back in without a fuss. He came briskly, he went briskly, and that was all. He didn't forget where he began; he didn't try to find out where he would end. He received something and took pleasure in it; he forgot about it and handed it back again. That is what I call not using the mind to repel the Way, not using man to help out Heaven. This is what I call the True Man.

Zhuangzi 6: 'The Great and Venerable Teacher'; Watson: 78

THE GREAT Clod (Earth) burdens me with form, labours me with life, eases me in old age, and rests me in death. So if I think well of my life, for the same reason I must think well of my death.

Zhuangzi 6: 'The Great and Venerable Teacher'; Watson: 80

WHILE YOU are alive, resign yourself and let life run its course; satisfy all your desires and wait for death. When it is time to die, resign yourself and let death run its course. Why need you delay it or speed it on its way?

Liezi 7: 'Yang Zhu'; Graham: 148

In contrast with later schools of Taoism such as the alchemists, the early masters did not believe in the value and methods of prolonging life and of even trying to reach physical immortality. If life and death are fated, why fight it?

'SUPPOSE THAT a man values his life and takes care of his body; may he hope by such means to live for ever?'
'It is impossible to live forever.'
'May he hope to prolong his life?'

'It is impossible to prolong life. Valuing life cannot preserve it, taking care of the body cannot do it good. Besides, what is the point of prolonging life? Our five passions, our likes and dislikes, are the same now as they were of old. The safety and danger of our four limbs, the joy and bitterness of worldly affairs, changes of fortune, good government and discord, are the same now as they were of old. We have heard it already, seen it already, experienced it already. Even a hundred years is enough to satiate us; could we endure the bitterness of still longer life?'

Liezi 7: 'Yang Zhu'; Graham: 147–8

'IT IS human to want long life and hate death. Why should you be happy to die?'
'Death is a return to where we set out from when we were born. So how do I know that when I die here I shall not be born somewhere else? How do I know that life and death are not as good as each other? How do I know that it is not a delusion to crave anxiously for life? How do I know that present death would not be better than my past life?'

Liezi 1: 'Heaven's Gifts'; Graham: 25

One of the most beautiful anecdotes in the Zhuangzi is the story of four gentlemen who become friends. Soon afterwards some of them became ill and were on the verge of dying. But death is seen here as the transformation of the life force; whereas it is the end of one's individuality, new life forms are continuously created. It is like a continuous firework, eternal in its whole, but finite in its individual expressions.

Several times the term 'Creator' occurs; the Chinese text does not point to a personal Creator, but to a 'Creative Force'.

MASTER SSU, Master Yü, Master Li, and Master Lai were all four talking together. 'Who can look upon non-being as his head, on life as his back, and on death as his rump?' they said. 'Who knows that life and death, existence and annihilation, are all a single body? I will be his friend!'

The four men looked at each other and smiled. There was no disagreement in their hearts and so the four of them became friends.

All at once Master Yü fell ill. Master Ssu went to ask how he was. 'Amazing!' said Master Yü. 'The Creator is making me all crookedy like this! My back sticks up like a hunchback and my vital organs are on top of me. My chin is hidden in my navel, my shoulders are up above my head, and my pigtail points at the sky. It must be some dislocation of the yin and yang!' Yet he seemed calm at heart and unconcerned. Dragging himself haltingly to the well, he looked at his reflection and said, 'My, my! So the Creator is making me all crookedy like this!'

'Do you resent it?' asked Master Ssu.

'Why no, what would I resent? If the process continues, perhaps in time he'll transform my left arm into a rooster. In that case I'll keep watch on the night. Or perhaps in time he'll transform my right arm into a crossbow pellet and I'll shoot down an owl for roasting. Or perhaps in time he'll transform my buttocks into cartwheels. Then, with my spirit for a horse, I'll climb up and go for a ride. What need will I ever have for a carriage again?

'I received life because the time had come; I will lose it because the order of things passes on. Be content with this time and dwell in this order and then neither sorrow nor joy can touch you. In ancient times this was called the "freeing of the bound". There are those who cannot free themselves, because they are bound by things. But nothing can ever win against Heaven – that's the way it's always been. What would I have to resent?'

Zhuangzi 6: 'The Great and Venerable Teacher'; Watson: 83–5

A continuation of the story is more specific as far as preserving one's individuality after death is concerned. There is no such thing! And demanding to become human again is pure arrogance.

SUDDENLY MASTER Lai grew ill. Gasping and wheezing, he lay at the point of death. His wife and children gathered round in a circle and began to cry. Master Li, who had come to ask how he was, said, 'Shoo! Get back! Don't disturb the process of change!'

Then he leaned against the doorway and talked to Master Lai. 'How marvellous the Creator is! What is he going to make of you next? Where is he going to send you? Will he make you into a rat's liver? Will he make you into a bug's arm?'

Master Lai said, 'A child, obeying his father and mother, goes wherever he is told, east or west, south or north. And the yin and yang – how much more are they to a man than father or mother! Now that they have brought me to the verge of death, if I should refuse to obey them, how perverse I would be! What fault is it of theirs? The Great Clod burdens me with form, labours me with life, eases me in old age, and rests me in death. So if I think well of my life, for the same reason I must think well of my death. When a skilled smith is casting metal, if the metal should leap up and say, "I insist upon being made into a Mo-yeh!" [a famous sword like Excalibur] he would surely regard it as very inauspicious metal indeed. Now, having had the audacity to take on human form once, if I should say, "I don't want to be anything but a man! Nothing but a man!", the Creator would surely regard me as a most inauspicious sort of person. So now I think of heaven and earth as a great furnace, and the Creator as a skilled smith. Where could he send me that would not be all right? I will go off to sleep peacefully, and then with a start I will wake up.'

Zhuangzi 6: 'The Great and Venerable Teacher'; Watson: 85

If life and death are like two sides of one coin, it does not make much sense, for a Taoist, to go into mourning when someone near us passes away (see also 'Life and Death are Fated' and 'Destiny and Human Effort').

WHEN LAO Dan died, Qin Shi went to mourn for him; but after giving three cries, he left the room.

'Weren't you a friend of the Master?' asked Laozi's disciples.

'Yes.'

'And you think it's all right to mourn him this way?'

'Yes,' said Qin Shi. 'At first I took him for a real man, but now I know he wasn't. A little while ago, when I went in to mourn, I found old men weeping for him as though they were weeping for a son, and young men weeping for him as though they were weeping for a mother. To have gathered a group like that, he must have done something to make them talk about him, though he didn't ask them to talk, or make them weep for him, though he didn't ask them to weep. This is to hide from Heaven, turn your back on the true state of affairs, and forget what you were born with. In the old days, this was called the crime of hiding from Heaven. Your master happened to come because it was his time, and he happened to leave because things follow along. If you are content with the time and willing to follow along, then grief and joy have no way to enter in.

Zhuangzi 3: 'The Secret of Caring for Life'; Watson, 52–3

DYING IS GOING TO REST

Life passes through four stages, similar to the year's four seasons: infancy, youth, old age, death. There is nothing strange about it, as the Daodejing *states that all living beings flourish for a while and then return to their roots.*

FROM HIS birth to his end, man passes through four great changes: infancy, youth, old age, death. In infancy his energies are concentrated and his inclinations at one – the ultimate of harmony. Other things do not harm him, nothing can add to the virtue in him. In youth, the energies in his blood are in turmoil and overwhelm him, desires and cares rise up and fill him. Others attack him, therefore the virtue wanes in him. When he is old, desires and cares weaken, his body is about to rest. Nothing contends to get ahead of him, and although he has not reached the perfection of infancy, compared with his youth there is a great difference for the better. When he dies, he goes to his rest, rises again to his zenith.

Liezi 1: 'Heaven's Gifts'; Graham: 23

ZIGONG GREW weary of study, and told Confucius: 'I want to find rest.'

'There is no rest for the living.'

'Then shall I never find it?'

'You shall. Look forward to the lofty and domed mound of your tomb, and know where you shall find rest.'

'Great is death! The gentleman finds rest in it, the mean man submits to it!'

'Zigong, you have understood. All men understand the joy of being alive, but not its misery, the weariness of growing old but not its ease, the ugliness of death but not its repose.'

Liezi 1: 'Heaven's Gifts'; Graham: 26

YANZI SAID: 'How well the men of old understood death! The good find rest in it, the wicked submit to it.' Dying is the virtue in us going to its destination. The men of old called a dead man 'a man who has gone back.' Saying that the dead have gone back they implied that the living are travellers. The traveller who forgets to go back is a man who mistakes his home.

Liezi 1: 'Heaven's Gifts'; Graham: 26

VALUING LIFE, NOURISHING LIFE

The Taoist masters, in general, value life as the most precious gift and encourage nourishing it, so that one may live out the lifespan allotted by destiny. Some masters, however, are more sceptical: our efforts make no difference. Let's listen to both opinions.

VALUING LIFE cannot preserve it, taking care of the body cannot do it good; scorning life cannot shorten it, neglecting the body cannot do it harm. Hence some who value life do not live, some who scorn it do not die, some who take care of the body do it no good, some who neglect it do it no harm. This seems unreasonable, but it is not; in these cases life and death, good and harm, come of themselves.

Liezi 6: 'Endeavor and Destiny'; Graham: 129

HE WHO has mastered the true nature of life does not labour over what life cannot do. He who has mastered the true nature of fate does not labour over what knowledge cannot change. He who wants to nourish his body must first of all turn to things. And yet it is possible to have more than enough things and for the body still to go unnourished. He who has life must first of all see to it that it does not leave the body. And yet it is possible for life never to leave the body and still fail to be preserved. The coming of life cannot be fended off, its departure cannot be stopped. How pitiful the men of the world, who think that simply nourishing the body is enough to preserve life! But if nourishing the body is in the end not enough to preserve life, then why is what the world does worth doing? It may not be worth doing, and yet it cannot be left undone – this is unavoidable.

Zhuangzi 19: 'Mastering Life'; Watson: 197

The Zhuangzi describes various categories of practitioners all pursuing their private goals: either to be recluses or to engage in worldly affairs to improve the world. They are all judged as missing the essence. Here is the type of person who wants to prolong life:

TO PANT, to puff, to hail, to sip, to spit out the old breath and draw in the new, practising bear-hangings and bird stretchings, longevity his only concern – such is the life favoured by the scholar who practises Induction [Gymnastics], the man who nourishes his body, who hopes to live to be as old as Pengzu [mythical person who lived more than 860 years].

But to attain loftiness without constraining the will; to achieve moral training without benevolence and righteousness, good order without accomplishments of fame, leisure without rivers and seas, long life without Induction; to lose everything and yet possess everything, at ease in the illimitable, . . . This is the Way of Heaven and earth, the Virtue of the Sage. So it is said, Limpidity, silence, emptiness, inaction – these are the level of Heaven and earth, the substance of the Way and its Virtue.

Zhuangzi 15: 'Constrained in Will'; Watson: 167–8

The Daodejing *is less explicit with regard to valuing and nourishing life. Yet there are some indications that a long life is preferable to a short one. In fact, destiny seems to have its role to play. Out of ten people, only one person is destined for longevity:*

> AS SOON as one is born, one enters death.
> Out of ten, three march toward life.
> Out of ten, three march toward death.
> Of those who [should] live [but] hurry toward their
>   death-spot,
>   there are also three out of ten.
> Why is that? Because they live a too intense life.
> One hears that one who is good at
>   taking care of life, does encounter
>   neither rhinoceros nor tiger while travelling;
> Is not touched by weapons during battle.
> A rhinoceros finds no spot to butt its horns.
> A tiger finds no spot to pierce its claws.
> Weapons find no spot to thrust their blades.
> Why is that?
> Because in him there is no death-spot.

Daodejing 50

TO PROLONG life is called fortunate,
To direct the vital energy (*qi*) with one's mind is called
    strength.
All beings flourish and grow old:
    to force it is against the Tao.

Daodejing 55

Life is a precious gift to be cherished and to be treated with great care. A marvellous Zhuangzi story compares nourishing life with a butcher's extreme caution when he uses his butchering knife.

COOK DING was cutting up an ox for Lord Wenhui. At every touch of his hand, every heave of his shoulder, every move of the feet, every thrust of his knee – zip! zoop! He slithered the knife along with a zing and all was in perfect rhythm. . . .

'Ah, this is marvellous!' said Lord Wenhui. 'Imagine skill reaching such heights!'

Cook Ding laid down his knife and replied: 'What I care about is the Way, which goes beyond skill. . . . [after years of practice], I go at it by spirit and don't look with my eyes.

Perception and understanding have come to a stop and spirit moves where it wants.

A good cook changes his knife once a year – because he cuts. A mediocre cook changes his knife once a month – because he hacks. I've had this knife of mine for nineteen years and I've cut up thousands of oxen with it, and yet the blade is as good as though it had just come from the grindstone. . . .'

'Excellent!' said Lord Wenhui. 'I have heard the words of Cook Ding and learned how to care for life!'

Zhuangzi 3: 'The Secret of Caring for Life'; Watson: 50–1

PHYSICAL IMPAIRMENT VS. SPIRIT

IN LU there was a man named Shushan No-toes who had had his foot cut off. Stumping along, he went to see Confucius.

'You weren't careful enough!' said Confucius. 'Since you've already broken the law and got yourself into trouble like this, what do you expect to gain by coming to me now?'

No-Toes said, 'I just didn't understand my duty and was too careless of my body, and so I lost a foot. But I've come now because I still have something that is worth more than a foot and I want to try to hold on to it. There is nothing that heaven doesn't cover, nothing that earth doesn't bear up. I supposed, Master, that you would be like heaven and earth. How did I know you would act like this?'

'It was stupid of me,' said Confucius. 'Please Sir, won't you come in? I'd like to describe to you what I have learned.'

But No-Toes went out. . . .

No-Toes told the story to Lao Dan. 'Confucius certainly hasn't reached the stage of a Perfect Man has he? What does he mean coming around so obsequiously to study with you? He is after the sham illusion of fame and reputation and doesn't know that the Perfect Man looks on these as so many handcuffs and fetters!'

Lao Dan said, 'Why don't you just make him see that life and death are the same story, that acceptable and unacceptable are on a single string? Wouldn't it be well to free him from his handcuffs and fetters?'

No-Toes said, 'When Heaven has punished him, how can you set him free?'

Zhuangzi 5: 'The Sign of Virtue Complete'; Watson: 71–2

ENJOYING LIFE

Life is a free gift: it is natural to receive it with joy and to enjoy it. The Taoist masters of old all agree on this. Yang Zhu, who lived in the fourth century BCE, is a Taoist run wild. It is more accurate not to call him a Taoist at all, but an Epicurean in the strict sense. The Liezi, *however, contains a chapter on Yang Zhu, and it is to our advantage to hear his provocative views.*

WHAT IS man to live for? Where is he to find happiness? Only in fine clothes and good food, music and beautiful women.

Some in ten years, some in a hundred, we all die; saints and sages die, the wicked and foolish die. In life they were Yao and Shun [model sages of old], in death they are rotten bones; in life they were Jie and Zhou [reputed evil-doers], in death they are rotten bones. Rotten bones are all the same, who can tell them apart? Make haste to enjoy your life while you have it; why care what happens when you are dead?

Liezi 7: 'Yang Chu'; Graham: 139–40

Yang Zhu was also a realist: it is realistic to enjoy what one has and not to hanker for more. (See 'Contentment'.)

CONTENTMENT

The ancient masters warn us against desires running wild. A ruler governed by desires for power and wealth is a disaster for the country. A sage is able to overcome desire and be content. Contentment is the precious jewel of happiness.

A GRAND HOUSE, fine clothes, good food, beautiful women – if you have these four, what more do you need from outside yourself? One who has them yet seeks more from outside himself has an insatiable nature. An insatiable nature is a grub eating away one's vital forces.

Liezi 6: 'Yang Chu'; Graham: 156

IT IS said, those who shepherded the world in ancient times were without desires and the world was satisfied, without action and the ten thousand things were transformed. They were deep and silent and the hundred clans were at rest.

Zhuangzi 12: 'Heaven and Earth'; Watson: 127

Desire for power is the cause of war in the case of rulers; the cause of calamity in the case of individuals. There is only one antidote to it: contentment.

THERE IS no greater calamity than not to know
     contentment.
There is no greater disaster than always to desire for
     more.
Indeed: who knows the contentment of being content,
     is always content.

Daodejing 46

A DWELLING filled with gold and jade
     will not long remain safe.
Pride over wealth and honour
     is the cause of collapse.

Daodejing 9

WHOEVER IS always without desires,
    is able to penetrate into the sublimity [of the Tao]
Whoever always has desires,
    can only contemplate the [Tao's] externals.

Daodejing 1

WHAT IS difficult to obtain in the world is neither wealth nor honour. It is knowing contentment. What worries people is the endless flow of desire.

JI KANG [Three Kingdoms Period]: *Da xiangzi yinan yangshenglun;* trans. J. Pas, from *Dictionary of Famous Quotations*: 417

THOSE WHO know contentment, are in oneness with the Tao and its power. They renounce fame and profit, and make themselves stand up within the realm of emptiness.

YAN ZUN [Han dynasty]: *Daode chiguilun;* trans. J. Pas from *Dictionary of Famous Quotations*: 417

THE SAGE-RULER

THE SAGE: APEX OF HUMAN PERFECTION

In the Daodejing, *the term for one who has reached perfection is* shengren: *sage (or saint). In the* Zhuangzi *several other terms are used, probably as equivalents:* zhenren *(the true person; the realized man);* shenren *(the spiritual person, the holy man);* zhiren *(the perfect person, the utmost man).*

In later religious texts of Taoism, the ideal most commonly aspired to is expressed by xian, *variously translated as 'immortal, perfected, transcendent'. To become a* xian, *one must follow a rigorous programme of spiritual and physical practices. (See under 'Immortal'.)*

> THE SAGE holds on to Oneness
> and becomes the model in the land.
> He does not display himself and thus shines.
> He does not justify himself and thus is known all
> around.
> He does not show off and thus receives credit.
> He does not brag and thus lasts long.
> Precisely because he does not compete, nobody in the
> land can compete with him.
>
> *Daodejing 22*

THE SAGE acts but is not over-confident;
  he achieves but does not dwell in it.
He has no desire to show his excellence.

Daodejing 77

H IS LIFE is the very course of nature; his death, the transformation of things. In quietude, he coils up with the yin; in movement, he opens up with the yang. His vital spirits are imbued with an endless peace, he does not lose himself in things and yet the world spontaneously submits to him. . . . By non-being the sage responds to things and necessarily penetrates into the laws of existence; by his emptiness he receives the plenitude and necessarily fathoms its rules. Calm and unconscious, empty and peaceful, he thus fulfils his destiny. Therefore, nothing is distant from him, nothing is close to him, he embraces *De* and blends with Harmony, and follows thereby the course of heaven. He is close to Tao and touches *De*, he is not enticed by good fortune, nor does he hasten into misfortune; his *hun* and *po* (souls) remain in their dwelling places and his vital spirits hold on to the root. Life and death make no difference to him; that is why he is called supremely spiritual (*shen*, divine).

Huainanzu 7; Robinet: 42

The Sage: Apex of Human Perfection ← 95

HE WHO holds fast to the Way is complete in Virtue (*De*); being complete in Virtue, he is complete in body; being complete in body, he is complete in spirit (*shen*) and to be complete in spirit is the Way of the sage. He is content to live among the people, to walk by their side, and never know where he is going. Witless, his purity is complete. Achievement, profit, machines, skill – they have no place in this man's mind! A man like this will not go where he has no will to go, will not do what he has no mind to do. . . .

The praise and blame of the world are no loss or gain to him. He may be called a man of Complete Virtue.

Zhuangzi 12: 'Heaven and Earth'; Watson: 135–6

THE SAGE embraces all heaven and earth, and his bounty extends to the whole world, yet no one knows who he is or what family he belongs to. For this reason, in life he holds no titles, in death he receives no posthumous names. Realities do not gather about him, names do not stick to him – this is what is called the Great Man.

Zhuangzi 24: 'Xu Wugui'; Watson: 272

It has already been said that human perfection is indicated by a variety of terms besides the term shengren. *Here follow some of the alternatives. The man of spirit,* shenren *(or spiritual person)* . . .

L ETS HIS spirit ascend and mount upon the light; with his bodily form he dissolves and is gone. This is called the Illumination of Vastness. He lives out his fate, follows to the end his true form, and rests in the joy of Heaven and earth, while the ten thousand cares melt away. So all things return to their true form. This is called Muddled Darkness.

Zhuangzi 12: 'Heaven and Earth'; Watson: 137

THE PERFECT Man [*zhiren*] has no self;
The Holy Man [*shenren*] has no merit;
The Sage [*shengren*] has no fame.

Zhuangzi 1: 'Free Flight into Transcendence'; Watson: 32

THE SAGE'S TRANSCENDENCE

The Zhuangzi starts with a tall story of a mythical fish that changes into a mythical bird: symbol of the sage's transcendence. The bird's flight goes far beyond the capacity of small creatures. Likewise, the sage transcends the myriad small creatures with little understanding. The huge bird also symbolizes the sage's mystical wanderings beyond time and space: it is a state of spiritual freedom and perfection.

I N THE northern darkness there is a fish and his name is Kun. The Kun is so huge I don't know how many thousand *li* he measures. He changes and becomes a bird whose name is Peng. The back of the Peng measures I don't know how many thousand *li* across and, when he rises up and flies off, his wings are like clouds all over the sky. When the sea begins to move, this bird sets off for the southern darkness, the waters are roiled for three thousand *li*. He beats the whirlwind and rises ninety thousand *li*, setting off on the sixth-month gale. . . .

If water is not piled up deep enough, it won't have the strength to bear up a big boat. Pour a cup of water into a hollow in the floor and bits of trash will sail on it like boats . . .

If wind is not piled up deep enough, it won't have the strength to bear up great wings. Therefore when the Peng rises ninety thousand *li*, he must have the wind under him like that. Only then can he mount on the back of the wind, shoulder the blue sky and nothing can hinder or block him. Only then can he set his eyes to the south.

The cicada and little dove laugh at this, saying: 'When we make an effort and fly up, we can get as far as the sapanwood tree, but sometimes we don't make it and just fall down on the ground. Now how is anyone going to go ninety thousand *li* to the south!' . . .

What do these two creatures understand? Little understanding cannot come up to great understanding; the short-lived cannot come up to the long-lived. . . .

We can't expect a blind man to appreciate beautiful patterns or a deaf man to listen to bells and drums. And blindness and deafness are not confined to the body alone – the understanding has them too.

Zhuangzi 1: 'Free Flight into Transcendence'; Watson: 29–33

ACTION OF THE SAGE

The sage is a person in union with the Tao. His/her mode of operation follows the pattern of the Tao, which is ultimately 'non-action' (wuwei).

IN HIS actions the sage practises 'non-action',
He spreads the teaching of 'not speaking'.
All beings flourish increasingly and he does not reject
   them.
He generates but does not possess.
He acts but does not grasp.
He brings to completion but is not attached.
Precisely because he is not attached, he loses nothing.

Daodejing 2

THE SAGE keeps himself in the background,
   but finds himself in the foreground.
He eliminates his own person,
   but his personality stands firm.
Is it not because he is selfless
   that his identity is realized?

Daodejing 7

THE SAGE avoids extremes
   he avoids empty show,
   he avoids excesses.

Daodejing 29

THE SAGE knows without travelling,
   understands without seeing,
   accomplishes without acting.

Daodejing 47

THE SAGE makes square without cutting,
Rounds off the corners without injuring,
Straightens without stretching to excess,
Shines without dazzling.

Daodejing 58

THE SAGE does not act and does not spoil.
He does not grasp and does not lose.

The sage desires not to desire;
He does not evaluate rare objects.
He learns the not-learning,
Repairs what the multitude has done wrong.
Since he supports the self-nature of all beings,
He does not dare to act.

Daodejing 64

THE SAGE knows himself, but does not show himself.
He loves himself, but does not value himself.

Daodejing 72

THE SAGE does not accumulate:
> The more he acts for others, the more he has himself;
> The more he gives to others, the more he possesses himself.

The way of the sage is to act but not to compete.

Daodejing 81

THE SAGE-RULER

Ideally, the person who rules the country is a sage. This comes through very clearly in the Daodejing, *where the figure of the sage often appears outside the context of government, but is also often pictured as a ruler, indeed as the ideal ruler: a sage-ruler.*

The Daodejing *occasionally shows an anti-intellectual tendency: to keep the people ignorant while making sure there is plenty of food, is presented as the best method of maintaining harmony in the state.*

Zhuangzi, on the other hand, scorns government and discourages others from accepting government appointments: it is too dangerous, for kings are known to be unpredictable.

THE GOVERNMENT of the sage consists in emptying the
    minds and filling the belly,
In weakening ambitions and strengthening the bones.
If he constantly keeps the people ignorant and
    desireless,
He will prevent the crafty ones from daring to act.
By practising non-action, there will be nothing that is
    not ordered.

Daodejing 3

THE SAGE does not have a constant mind:
>   he regards the people's minds as his own. . . .
The presence of the sage in the land brings harmony:
>   his mind goes out to the land.
The people all centre their eyes and ears on him:
>   the sage treats them all as his children.

Daodejing 49

RULE THE country with correctness.
Deploy the army with surprise strategy.
Hold on to (win) the land by not engaging in action.
How do I know this is so? By this:
The more taboos there are in the land,
>   the more impoverished the people are.
The more the people possess sharp weapons,
>   the greater the country's confusion.
The more cunning the people are,
>   the more extraordinary things appear.
The more laws are promulgated,
>   the more thieves there are.
Therefore the sage says:
I do not act and the people are transformed of themselves.

Daodejing 57

IN GOVERNING the people and serving heaven
nothing is better than frugality.

Daodejing 60

GOVERNING A large state is like frying small fish.
[*Too much manipulation spoils it.*]

Daodejing 60

IF A large state places itself below a small state,
it can win the small state.
If a small state places itself below a large state,
it can win the large state. . . .
Whoever wishes to be great,
does well to lower himself.

Daodejing 61

WHOEVER DESIRES to be above the people,
  must be below them in his words.
Whoever desires to be ahead of the people,
  must be behind them in his own person.
As a result the sage stands above the people,
  but they do not feel it as a burden.
He is ahead of the people,
  but they do not experience any harm. . . .
Because he does not compete, no one in the land can
  compete with him.

Daodejing 66

IF THE ruler is limpid, still, and non-active,
the heavens will provide him with the proper seasons.
If he does not appropriate what is not his,
is frugal, and keeps to moderation,
the earth will yield him up its bounty.
If he is content with being stupid while praising
the virtues of others,
sages will lend him their counsel.
It is to the low ground that the myriad things repair
and to the empty that the empire gives its gifts.

Huainanzi, Book 9: 'The Art of Rulership'; trans. Ames: 178

THE WAY of the ruler is to cultivate his person by dwelling in quietude and to lead his subjects with frugality and moderation. If he is quiet, his subjects are not disturbed; if he is frugal, his people will have no cause to complain. Should his subjects be disturbed it would mean political disorder; should his people have cause to complain, it would mean that his bounty is not generous. Where there is political disorder, those of superior character will not proffer their counsel, and where the ruler's bounty is not generous, those of valour will not die for him.

Huainanzi, Book 9: 'The Art of Rulership'; trans. Ames: 186

THE CLEVER man gives responsibility to others, and therefore his power does not diminish when he grows old, and he is not thrown into confusion when his knowledge runs out. Therefore the difficulty in ruling a state lies in recognizing cleverness, not in being clever oneself.

Liezi 8: 'Explaining Conjunctions'; Graham: 161

Kᴵᴺᴳ ᶻᴴᵁᴬᴺᴳ of Chu asked Zhan He:

'How shall I put my state in order?'

'Your servant understands how to put one's own life in order, but not the state.'

'I have inherited the shrines of my royal ancestors and the altars of the state; I wish to learn how to keep them.'

'Your servant has never heard of a prince whose own life was in order yet his state in turmoil, nor of any whose life was in turmoil but his state in order. Therefore the root lies in your government of yourself; I would not presume to answer you by talking of the tips of the branches.'

'Good!' said the King of Chu.

Liezi 8: 'Explaining Conjunctions'; Graham: 170–1

A GIFT TO THE RULER

When rulers are enthroned and officials are installed, they receive many precious gifts, such as jade and chariots. There is one gift more precious than anything else.

WHEN THE son of heaven [emperor] is enthroned,
or when the three dukes are installed,
although jade tablets are presented
preceded by teams of horses,
it would be better to kneel before them
    and to offer this Tao.

Daodejing 62

THERE IS ALSO BAD GOVERNMENT!

Rulers are tempted by desire for power and wealth. Unless they practise frugality and thrift, the people will be poor and will suffer.

THE COURTS are kept in good shape,
    but the fields are filled with weeds;
    the granaries are empty.
They [the rulers] are dressed in colourful silks,
    they carry sharp swords,
    are saturated with food and drink;
    wealth and goods are abundant.
This is called robbery and showing off.
It is not at all the Tao!

Daodejing 53

THE PEOPLE suffer starvation because the rulers eat too
   much tax-grain.
   That is why they starve.
The people are hard to govern because the rulers act
   [interfere] too much.
   That is why they are hard to govern.
The people take death lightly, because the rulers live
   too intensely.
   That is why they take death lightly.
Only those who do 'not act' in order to live are
   eminent in valuing life.

Daodejing 75

I F THE ruler has a penchant for predatory birds and ferocious
animals, rare and exotic things, and is anxious and agitated,
if he is not sparing with the efforts of his people, enjoys
horses and hunting and takes to the field at whatever time he
pleases, then the duties of bureaucracy will be thrown into
disorder and there will be little material wealth in spite of
hard work, the people will be miserable and distressed, and
their means of livelihood will go untended. Where the ruler is
fond of high pavilions, deep ponds, sculptured and engraved
ornamentation, beautifully colourful patterns, fine lines and
embroidery, precious stones and jewels, then his taxes will be
exorbitant and the energies of the common people will be
utterly depleted.

Huainanzi, Book 9: 'The Art of Rulership'; trans. Ames:
186–7

MILITARY STRATEGY

In ancient China, warfare was a very common government 'hobby', often engaged in for flimsy reasons. The Taoists, however, opposed war and would only approve of it in case of outside attack. Even then, killing others was seen as regrettable. Victory in war was seen as a funeral service.

HE WHO wants to assist the leader of men with the Tao,
    does not coerce the land through military force.
Military force easily leads to revenge.
Wherever armies are stationed, thistles and thorns
    grow.
After a fierce battle, bitter years are certain to follow.
A good [general] accomplishes his task and stops;
He accomplishes his mission but does not show off;
He accomplishes his mission but does not brag;
He accomplishes his mission but is not proud of it;
He accomplishes his mission but with reluctance;
He accomplishes his mission but does not coerce.

Daodejing 30

FINE WEAPONS are instruments of evil omen;
  many people hate them.
Therefore, a man of Tao dislikes them. . . .
Weapons are instruments of evil omen,
  not the instruments of a good prince.
He uses them with reluctance. . . .
To praise a victory is to find pleasure in the slaughter
  of people.
Who finds pleasure in the slaughter of people
  will not realize his plans in the land. . . .
Since in war many lost their lives,
  one should shed tears of sorrow and mourning.
During a celebration of victory, one should place
  the people as during a funeral.

Daodejing 31

IF THE Tao prevails in the land,
   one withdraws the horses for their dung.
If the Tao fails in the land,
   warhorses are bred in the suburbs.

Daodejing 46

IF ONE has compassionate love in battle,
   one will win victory.
In defence, one will hold out.
If heaven wants to save someone, it will protect
   him because of compassionate love.

Daodejing 67

A GOOD leader of men is not aggressive.
A good warrior does not get angry.
A good victor does not compare.
A good employer of men places himself below.
This is called the power of not competing.

Daodejing 68

A STRATEGIST of old has said:
  'I dare not be the aggressor but rather the defender;
  I dare not advance an inch but rather retreat a foot.'
  . . .
There is no greater calamity than to underestimate
  one's enemy. . . .
When arms are lifted in mutual clash,
  victory is to those who grieve.

Daodejing 69

WHO HAS the courage to dare, will be killed.
Who has the courage not to dare, will live.

Daodejing 73

WUWEI: TAKING NO ACTION

One of the greatest paradoxes of early Taoist thought is the concept of wuwei, *literally 'non-action'. It does not mean that governments do nothing, but that they interfere as little as possible in the lives of the people. Let the people take the initiative, and society will run smoothly. Interference is counter-productive; it causes unrest and may even lead to open rebellion.*

In an applied sense, wuwei is also important in the lives of individuals. Here it means to let others alone, not to force them to think and act against their own selves, not to put claims on them, not to expect rewards for one's services. It also means that one does not own anybody, not even one's dearest ones. Love must be a free gift: one cannot demand it.

The richness of the wuwei *concept is truly amazing; its applications in real life never end.*

> FEW UNDER heaven come up to the principle of wordless
> teaching,
> and the advantages of non-action.

Daodejing 43

THE PURSUIT of learning is to increase everyday.
The pursuit of the Tao is to diminish everyday.
To diminish and again to diminish
    till one reaches the state of non-action.
No action takes place yet nothing is left undone.
By constantly not engaging in action
    one wins the land.
If one engages in action, one is not worth winning the
    land.

Daodejing 48

ACT WITHOUT acting.
Do without doing.
Taste without tasting.
Enlarge the small,
Increase the few.
Respond to resentment with kindness.
Plan the difficult when it's still easy.
Do the great while it's still small.
Therefore the sage never does the great,
And is then able to achieve greatness.

Daodejing 63

WIN THE land by not engaging in action. . . .
Therefore the sage says:
I do not act and the people are transformed of
   themselves.
I love tranquillity and the people order themselves.
I do not manage affairs and the people enrich
   themselves.
I have no desires and the people become whole by
   themselves.

Daodejing 57

IF SOMEONE wants to seize the land and manipulate it,
   I see that he will not succeed.
The land is something 'spiritual'. It cannot be
   manipulated.
To manipulate it is to destroy it.
   to grasp it is to lose it.

Daodejing 29

I T IS said [that] those who shepherded the world in ancient times were without desire and the world was satisfied, without action and the ten thousand things were transformed. They were deep and silent and the hundred clans were at rest.

Zhuangzi 12: 'Heaven and Earth'; Watson: 127

Wuwei has been interpreted in many ways. All interpretations reveal some aspects of it, but rarely have they touched upon all its angles. Here is one interpretation: the perfect person, who

R EMAINS WITHIN society but refrains from acting out of the motives that lead ordinary men to struggle for wealth, fame, success, or safety. He maintains a state [of] *wuwei*, or inaction, . . . a course of action that is not founded upon any purposeful motives of gain or striving. In such a state, all human actions become as spontaneous and mindless as those of the natural world.

Watson: 6

Zhuangzi, and Liezi after him, often use the analogy of the craftsman or artist to describe this mode of life.

WOODWORKER QING carved a piece of wood and made a bell stand, and when it was finished, everyone who saw it marvelled, for it seemed to be the work of gods or spirits. When the marquis of Lu saw it, he asked, 'What art is it you have?'

Qing replied, 'I am only a craftsman – how would I have any art? There is one thing, however. When I am going to make a bell stand, I never let it wear out my energy. I always fast in order to still my mind. When I have fasted for three days, I no longer have any thought of congratulations or rewards, of titles or stipends. When I have fasted for five days, I no longer have any thought of praise or blame, of skill or clumsiness. And when I have fasted for seven days, I am so still that I forget I have four limbs and a form and body. By that time, the ruler and his court no longer exist for me. My skill is concentrated and all outside distractions fade away. After that, I go into the mountain forest and examine the Heavenly nature of the trees. If I find one of superlative form, and I can see a bell stand there, I put my hand to the job of carving; if not, I let it go. This way I am simply matching up "Heaven" with "Heaven". That's probably the reason that people wonder if the results were not made by spirits.'

Zhuangzi 19: 'Mastering Life'; Watson: 205–6

If one is guided by ulterior motives to engage in selfish action, one might not succeed. The story of the seagulls speaks for itself.

THERE WAS a man living by the sea-shore who loved seagulls. Every morning he went down to the sea to roam with the seagulls, and more birds came to him than you could count in hundreds. His father said to him:

'I hear the seagulls all come roaming with you. Bring me some to play with.'

Next day, when he went down to the sea, the seagulls danced above him and would not come down.

Therefore, it is said: 'The utmost in speech is to be rid of speech, the utmost doing is Doing Nothing.'

Liezi 2: 'The Yellow Emperor'; Graham: 45–6

In Joseph Needham's monumental work, Science and Civilization in China, *one finds another interpretation of* wuwei *as:*

REFRAINING FROM activity contrary to Nature, i.e. from insisting on going against the grain of things, from trying to make materials perform functions for which they are unsuitable, from exerting force in human affairs when the men of insight could see that it would be doomed to failure, and that subtler methods of persuasion, or simply letting things alone to take their own course, would bring about the desired result.

Needham: II: 68

He quotes from the Huainanzi *to illustrate the point:*

SOME MAY maintain that the person who acts in the spirit of *wuwei* is one who is serene and does not speak, or one who meditates and does not move; he will not come when called nor be driven by force. And this demeanour, it is assumed, is the appearance of one who has obtained the Tao. Such an interpretation of *wuwei* I cannot admit. I never heard such an explanation from any sage . . .

The configuration of the earth causes water to flow eastward, nevertheless man must open channels for it to run in canals. Cereal plants sprout in spring, nevertheless it is necessary to add human labour in order to induce them to grow and mature. If everything were left to Nature, and birth and growth were awaited without human effort, Kun and Yü [ancient sages] would have acquired no merit, and the knowledge of Hou Ji [lord of grain, ancient agricultural folk-hero] would not have been put to use. What is meant, therefore, in my view, by *wuwei*, is that no personal prejudice interferes with the universe, and that no desires and obsessions lead the true courses of techniques astray. Reason must guide action, in order that power may be exercised according to the intrinsic properties and natural trends of things. . . .

The sages in all their methods of action, follow the Nature of Things.

Needham: II: 68–9

To sum up Needham says,

PLANTS GROW best without interference by man; men thrive best without state interference.

Needham:II: 70

In contrast to what the 'world' thinks, true happiness exists in taking no action. This is difficult to understand and to accept; one has to be a sage to accept and to practise it. However, one has to keep in mind that 'non-action' does not mean 'doing nothing'!

IS THERE such a thing as perfect happiness in the world or isn't there? Is there some way to keep yourself alive or isn't there? . . .

What ordinary people do and what they find happiness in – I don't know whether such happiness is in the end really happiness or not. I look at what ordinary people find happiness in, what they all make a mad dash for, racing around as though they can't stop – they all say they're happy with it. I'm not happy with it and I'm not unhappy with it. In the end is there really happiness or isn't there?

I take inaction to be true happiness, but ordinary people think it is a bitter thing. I say: perfect happiness knows no happiness, perfect praise knows no praise. The world can't decide what is right and what is wrong. And yet inaction can decide this. Perfect happiness, keeping alive – only inaction gets you close to this.

Let me try to put it this way. The inaction of Heaven is its purity, the inaction of earth is its peace. So the two inactions combine and all things are transformed and brought to birth. Mysteriously, wonderfully, they have no sign. Each thing minds its business and all grow up out of inaction. So I say, Heaven and earth do nothing and there is nothing that is not done. Among men, who can get hold of this inaction?

Zhuangzi 18: 'Perfect Happiness'; Watson: 190–1

MYSTICAL SPARKLES

Although the Daodejing *was written to guide rulers to conduct correct government, the text has definite mystical overtones. A good ruler must be in tune with the Tao, or better still, in deep union with the Tao realized through stillness of the senses and deep contemplation.*

The Zhuangzi *does not share the same ideal: a true sage turns his back on government, prefers to be 'useless', and wanders in transcendence beyond the common world of men. The* Zhuangzi's *ideal of the 'true person' is a mystic who has gained insight into the reality of the Tao and enjoys perfect freedom from constraints beyond normal comprehension.*

> IN HOLDING together the two vital forces ('souls'),
>   can you avoid letting them separate?
> In concentrating on *qi* and reaching weakness,
>   can you make it spotless?
> In purifying your mysterious vision (mirror),
>   can you become like an infant?

In loving the people and ruling the country,
    can you apply non-action?
In opening and closing the 'natural' gates,
    can you do it without the feminine?
In understanding the universe,
    can you remain without knowledge?

Daodejing 10

REACH COMPLETE emptiness,
    maintain the greatest calmness.

Daodejing 16

BLOCK UP the apertures,
    close the gates.
Till the end of life
    strength will not fail.

Open the apertures,
    engage in activities.
Till the end of life
    nothing will avail.

Daodejing 52

MAKE USE of the light.
Return to its brightness.
Do not expose yourself to danger.
This is cultivating the constant.

Daodejing 52

BLUNT THE sharpness.
Untangle the ties.
Harmonize with the light.
Become one with the dusty world.
This is mysterious identification.

Daodejing 4

THE ESSENCE of the Perfect Way [said Master Guang to the Yellow Emperor] is deep and darkly shrouded; the extreme of the Perfect Way is mysterious and hushed in silence. Let there be no seeing, no hearing; enfold the spirit in quietude and the body will right itself. Be still, be pure, do not labour your body, do not churn up your essence, and then you can live a long life. . . .

All the hundred creatures that flourish are born out of dust and return to dust. So I will take leave of you, to enter the gate of the inexhaustible and wander in the limitless fields, to form a triad with the light of the sun and moon, to partake in the constancy of Heaven and earth. What stands before me I mingle with. What is far from me I leave in darkness. All other men may die; I alone will survive!

Zhuangzi 11: 'Let it Be, Leave it Alone'; Watson: 117–20

THE SAGE is still not because he takes stillness to be good and therefore is still. The ten thousand things are insufficient to distract his mind – that is the reason he is still. Water that is still gives back a clear image of beard and eyebrows; reposing in the water level, it offers a measure to the great carpenter. And if water in stillness possesses such clarity, how much more must pure spirit. The sage's mind in stillness is the mirror of Heaven and earth, the glass of the ten thousand things.

Emptiness, stillness, limpidity, silence, inaction – these are the level of Heaven and earth, the substance of the Way and its Virtue. Therefore the emperor, the king, the sage rest in them. Resting they may be empty; empty, they may be full; and fullness is completion! . . .

In stillness you will be a sage, in action a king.

Zhuangzi 13: 'The Way of Heaven'; Watson: 142–3

YOU HAVE only to rest [said Big Concealment to Cloud Chief] in inaction and things will transform themselves. Smash your form and body, spit out hearing and eyesight. Forget you are a thing among other things, and you may join in great unity with the deep and boundless. Undo the mind, slough off spirit, be blank and soulless, and the ten thousand things one by one will return to the root.

Zhuangzi 11: 'Let it Be, Leave it Alone'; Watson: 122

In a dialogue between Confucius and his disciple, Yan Hui, the Taoist author ironically transforms Confucius into a Taoist sage. After a long discussion, Confucius concludes that nothing will help Yan Hui to be a good adviser to the king but 'fasting of the mind', which goes beyond ordinary fasting.

'MAY I ask what the fasting of the mind is?' Confucius said: 'Make your will one! Don't listen with your ears, listen with your mind. No, don't listen with your mind, but listen with your spirit. Listening stops with the ears, the mind stops with recognition, but spirit is empty and waits on all things. The Way gathers in emptiness alone. Emptiness is the fasting of the mind.'

Zhuangzi 4: 'In the World of Men'; Watson: 57–8

Concrete expressions of mystical rapture are rarely found in the Taoist texts. One impressive example is found in the Zhuangzi: it describes the gradual process of transcending the world and even oneself. A woman called Crookback explains how she tried to make a sage out of someone she recognized as having the 'talent of a sage'. (The text is somewhat paraphrased.)

> FIRST, (AFTER three days), he could put the world out of himself;
> Next, (after seven days), he could put things out of himself;
> Next, (after nine days), he could put life out of himself;
> Then, he could achieve the brightness of dawn;
> Then, he could see his own aloneness;
> Then he could do away with past and present;
> Then, finally, he could enter where there is no life or death.

Zhuangzi 6: 'The Great and Venerable Teacher'; Watson: 82–3

SPIRITUAL GROWTH

The theme of spiritual growth is probably the most common concern of all Taoist texts, both philosophical and religious. It is through control of the senses, inner meditation and visualization, appropriate diets, physical exercises, observance of ethical rules, and, moderately, alchemical experiments that a Taoist practitioner makes great efforts at spiritualizing his/her own person, and, in the Taoist religion, tries to reach the state of longevity/immortality.

In the earliest Taoist texts, spiritual growth is recommended to those who wish to become worthy rulers of the country. In the Zhuangzi, spiritual growth is its own goal: it brings about a state of perfection and happiness, freedom from all constraints.

As one can imagine, this theme overlaps with several others.

THE WAY is what the mouth cannot speak of
The eyes cannot look at
And the ears cannot listen to.
It is that by which we cultivate the mind and align the
    body.
It is what a person loses and thereby dies,
    What a person gains and is thereby born.

When undertakings lose it they fail;
     When they get it they succeed. . . .
The myriad things are born by means of it
     and by means of it develop
We name it 'Way'.

> *Guanzi,* 'Neiye'; trans. H. Roth in Lopez: 130

BY CONCENTRATING your vital energy as if numinous,
     the myriad things will all be contained within you.
Can you concentrate? Can you unify [your
     awareness]?
Can you know good and bad fortune without
     resorting to divination?

Can you stop? Can you halt?
Can you not seek it without, but attain it within? . . .
You think, yet still cannot penetrate it.
The demonic and numinous in you will penetrate it.
When the four limbs are correctly adjusted and the
     blood and vital energy are tranquil,
Unify your awareness, concentrate your mind
     and the eyes and ears will not be overstimulated.

> *Guanzi,* 'Neiye'; trans. H. Roth in Lopez: 132–3

HEAVEN IS said to be empty,
Earth is said to be tranquil.
And so they do not waiver.
Clean out its dwelling.
Open its doors,
Relinquish selfishness,
Avoid speaking.
Then the numinous light will be as if present.
When one is confused it (the mind) seems chaotic.
Still it and it will naturally become ordered.

Guanzi, 'Xinshu'; trans. H. Roth in Lopez: 136

HAPPINESS AND anger are aberrations of the Way.
Worry and sadness are lapses of inner power.
Likes and dislikes are excesses of the mind.
Lusts and desires are the fetters of one's nature.
In a human being:
>   Great anger damages the yin.
>   Great joy collapses the yang.
>   Weak vital energy causes dumbness.
>   Shock and fright bring about madness.
>   When worry, sadness, and rage abound,
>   Illnesses develop.
>   When likes and dislikes abound,
>   Misfortunes follow one another.
Thus
>   When the mind does not worry or rejoice,
>   This is the perfection of inner power.
>   When it is absorbed and does not alter,
>   This is the perfection of stillness.
>   When lusts and desires do not fill it up,
>   This is the perfection of emptiness.
>   When there is nothing liked or disliked,
>   This is the perfection of equanamity.
>   When it is not confused by external things,
>   This is the perfection of purity.

Those who are able to practise these five will be
   absorbed in the numinous light. Those who are
   absorbed in the numinous light are those who
   actualize what is within them.

   Guanzi, 'Xinshu'; trans. H. Roth in Lopez: 138

STILLNESS AND quietude, placidity and tranquillity,
Are the means by which we nourish our nature.
Harmony and serenity, emptiness and nothingness,
When the external does not confuse the internal,
Are the means by which we nourish inner power.
Then our nature will attain what is suitable to it.
When one's nature does not move from this harmony,
Then inner power secures its position.
To nourish the nature and thereby pass through one's
   generation,
To embrace inner power and thereby last out one's
   years,
Can be called 'being able to embody the Way'.

   Guanzi, 'Xinshu'; trans. H. Roth in Lopez:140–1

Often the Taoist masters, from the Guanzi *to the* Daodejing *and the* Zhuangzi, *emphasize the necessity of controlling the senses, of controlling one's passions and emotions. Lack of control is disastrous for one's spiritual growth.*

WHEN THE chest and belly are replete
And lusts and desires are eliminated
Then the ears and eyes are clear
And hearing and vision are acute.
When the ears and eyes are clear
And hearing and vision are acute,
We call this 'illumination'.

Guanzi, 'Xinshu'; trans. H. Roth in Lopez: 142

NOW THE sense apertures
And the vital energy and attention
Are the portals of the numinous essence
And the vital energy and attention
Are the servants of the Five Viscera [the inner organs].
When the eyes and ears
Are enticed by the pleasures of sound and color,
Then the Five Viscera oscillate and we are not stable.
When the Five Viscera oscillate and are not stable,

Then the blood and vital energy are agitated and not at
    rest.
When the blood and vital energy are agitated and not
    at rest,
Then the numinous essence courses out [through the
    eyes
    and ears] and is not preserved. . . .
But if you make:
    Your ears and eyes totally clear and profoundly
        penetrating,
    And you do not let them be enticed by external
        things,
    Your vital energy and attention empty,
        tranquil, still, and serene,
    And you eliminate lusts and desires;
    Your Five Viscera stable, reposed, replete, and full,
    And you do not let their vital energies leak out;
    Your numinous essence stays within your bodily
        frame,
    And you do not let it flow out:
Then you will be able to gaze before past generations
And to see beyond future events.

Guanzi, 'Xinshu'; trans. H. Roth in Lopez: 143–4

The danger of losing control of the senses is pointed out in very similar ways in a Guanzi *passage and in a* Daodejing *chapter. This suggests the possible influence of the* Guanzi *on the* Daodejing:

> THE FIVE colours disrupt the eyes
> And cause them to be unclear;
> The five sounds confuse the ears
> And cause them to not be acute;
> The five tastes disrupt the mouth
> And cause it to lose the ability to taste;
> Preferences confuse the mind
> And cause it to fly [from one thing to the next] . . .
> Thus it is said:
> Lusts and desires
> Dissipate a person's vital energy.
> And likes and dislikes
> Belabour a person's mind.

Guanzi, 'Xinshu'; trans. H. Roth in Lopez: 144

THOSE WE call the Genuine are people whose natures are
    united with the Way. Therefore:
    They possess it but appear to have nothing,
    They are filled by it but appear to be empty.
They rest in this unity
And know not duality.
They concentrate on what is inside
And pay no attention to what is outside.
They illuminate the great simplicity
And, without acting, revert to the unknown.
They embody the foundation and embrace the numen
And so roam freely through the turmoil of Heaven and
    Earth.
Untrammelled,
They ramble outside this dusty world
And wander amidst effortless activity.
Unfettered and unhindered,
They harbour no contrived cleverness in their minds. . . .

Abruptly they come;
Suddenly they go.
Form like withered wood,
Mind like dead ashes
They forget their Five Viscera,
Throw off their physical frame,
Know without studying,
See without looking.
They complete without acting
And they discern without ordering. . . .
Vast and empty, they are tranquil and without worry. . . .
They rest in the territory of the vast
And roam in the land of the boundless. . . .
This is how their numinous essence is able to ascend to
the Way.
This is the roaming of the Genuine.

Guanzi, 'Xinshu'; trans. H. Roth in Lopez: 146–8

It is amazing how many elements in this former text are echoed in the Zhuangzi *and the* Daodejing. *Among these parallels are references to 'great simplicity' (su) and 'the unhewn' (pu); to 'withered wood' and 'dead ashes'. 'Roaming in the land of the boundless' is one of Zhuangzi's favourite themes, expressing his ultimate freedom in mystical flight.*

Z IQI OF South Wall sat leaning on his armrest staring up at the sky and breathing – vacant and far away, . . . Yan, who was standing by his side in attendance, said, 'What is this? Can you really make the body like a withered tree and the mind like dead ashes? The man leaning on the armrest now is not the one who leaned on it before.'

Zhuangzi 2: 'The Equality of Things and Theories'; Watson: 36

The expressions 'withered wood' and 'dead ashes' are understood as indications of a state of rapture or mystical trance. They have a close affinity with another common expression 'sit and forget', describing a state of deep meditation. It is ironically one of Confucius' disciples, Yan Hui, who reports his experience. Twice he told his master he was improving, but Confucius said he still hadn't got it.

ANOTHER DAY, the two met again and Yan Hui said, 'I'm improving.'

'What do you mean by that?'

'I can sit down and forget everything!'

Confucius looked very startled and said: 'What do you mean, sit down and forget everything?'

Yan Hui said: 'I smash up my limbs and body, drive out perceptions and intellect, cast off form, do away with understanding and make myself identical with the Great Thoroughfare. This is what I mean by sitting down and forgetting everything.'

Zhuangzi 6: 'The Great and Venerable Teacher'; Watson: 90

MEDITATION

Several of the previous texts have clearly alluded to techniques of meditation. In many schools of Taoist practice, as in Buddhism (and perhaps under Buddhist influence) various meditation techniques have been developed through the ages. Perhaps the most sophisticated methods are products of the Shangqing (High Purity) School: one of them concerns concentration and visualization of the 'Inner Deities', whose assistance is necessary to have the adept's name transferred to the register of life.

One of the most significant texts was composed by Tang master Sima Chengzhen (647–735): Discourse on Sitting and Forgetting (Zuowanglun), *a practical and pedagogic instrument in the technique of meditation. Here follows a brief synopsis of the meditation process in seven stages:*

- RESPECT AND FAITH stresses a state of mind needed at the outset: trust in the method, freedom from doubt.
- INTERCEPTION OF KARMA explains the need to withdraw from ordinary life and leave all business outside. At least temporarily, the mind must be free from all worldly affairs and concerns.

- TURNING THE MIND brings home the urgent necessity of stilling the mind and reaching a state of 'blind concentration'. Only then can the mind be directed to its goal, in analogy with oxen and horses tamed and used by humans.
- DETACHMENT OF AFFAIRS goes even further by urging the inner separation from society and total detachment from worldly achievements.
- TRUE OBSERVATION (*zhenguan*) introduces the first stage of meditation, but rather than visualizing inner gods (*guan*), it involves concentration on one's situation, and a coming to grips with it.
- INTENT CONCENTRATION leads the adept to 'the first foothold of the Tao', which means 'perfect serenity on the inside and a "heavenly light" radiating on the outside' (Kohn: 37). It is like tranquillity and wisdom.
- REALIZING THE TAO explains how the mind is gradually emptied and united with the reality of Tao.

Summarized from Kohn, 1987a: 35–8

'Sitting in Oblivion' (zuowang) *is also discussed in Tang Master Sima Chengzhen's* Tianyinzi (The Master of Heavenly Seclusion), *mentioned earlier:*

THE INCREASING harmony of one's bodily functions with the Tao leads ultimately to a complete dissolution of any separate individual feeling of oneself. One 'forgets' oneself. Already the *Zhuangzi* describes this state: 'I smash up my limbs and body, [etc.]'

Guo Xiang adds: '. . . on the inside, one is unaware of one's personal body, on the outside, one never knows there is a universe.' The state that is entered here is a trance state. 'The body is like rotten wood, the mind is like dead ashes. There are no more impulses, no more search, one has reached perfect contemplative serenity.'

Tianyinzi; Kohn, 1987b: 23

WAYS TO IMMORTALITY

Whereas the Taoist masters Laozi and Zhuangzi do not speculate on life after death, nor advocate immortality of body-and-mind, the Taoist religion, at least in its monastic circles, developed methods of becoming an 'Immortal'. It involved rigorous practices of meditation, fasting and physical exercises, but also relied on the use of drugs (plant of immortality, life-enhancing elixirs, etc.) and techniques called 'inner alchemy', which aimed at purification of spirit and energy.

THE BODY is the habitation of spirit and energy. As long as spirit and energy are there, the body is healthy and strong. As soon as spirit and energy scatter, the body dies. Therefore, if you wish to preserve yourself whole, first calm spirit and energy.

Understand: energy is the mother of spirit; spirit is the son of energy. Only when energy and spirit are together can you live long and not die.

If you, therefore, wish to calm the spirit, first refine primordial energy. When this energy resides in the body, spirit is calm and energy is like an ocean. With the ocean of energy full to overflowing, the mind is calm and the spirit stable. When this stability is not scattered, body and mind are gathered in tranquillity. Tranquillity then attains to concentration, and the body continues to exist for years eternal.

Just stay all the time with the deep source of the Tao, and you will naturally become a sage. Then energy pervades spirit and all mental projections; spirit pervades all insight and destiny. With destiny established and the body preserved, you can unite both with your true inner nature. Then you will reach an age as old as the sun and the moon! Your Tao is perfected!

From the scripture *Visualization of Spirit and Refinement of Energy;* Kohn, 1993: 320–1

ALL PEOPLE from birth are endowed with the energy of emptiness. Originally their essence and enlightenment are of penetrating awareness, learning has no obstructions, and the 'spirit' is pure. Settle this spirit within and let it shine without! You will naturally become different from ordinary people. You will be a spirit immortal! Yet even as a spirit immortal, you are still human.

To accomplish spirit immortality you must cultivate the energy of emptiness. Never let the common world defile it. Find spirit immortality in spontaneously following your nature.

Never let false views obstruct your path.

Joy, anger, sadness, happiness, love, hate, and desires are the seven perversions of the emotions. Wind, damp, cold, heat, hunger, satiation, labour, and idleness are the eight perversions of energy. Rid yourself of them! Establish immortality!

From the scripture *The Master of Heavenly Seclusion;*
Kohn, 1993: 81

Progress on the way to immortality is gradual: there is no sudden enlightenment. There are five progressive gateways toward realizing the Tao. Reaching spirit immortality is expected at the end of the five steps.

THE FIRST is fasting and abstention.
The second is seclusion.
The third is visualization and imagination.
The fourth is sitting in oblivion.
The fifth is spirit liberation.

What does fasting and abstention mean? It means cleansing the body and emptying the mind.

What does seclusion mean? It means withdrawing deep into the meditation chamber.

What does visualization and imagination mean? It means taming the mind and recovering original nature.

What does sitting in oblivion mean? It means letting go of the personal body and completely forgetting oneself.

What does spirit liberation mean? It means spirit pervasion of all existence.

From the scripture *The Master of Heavenly Seclusion;*
Kohn, 1993: 82

L EAVING THE world does not mean that the body departs. Rather, it refers to the mind. The body is like the lotus root; the mind is like the lotus blossom. The root is in the mud, yet the blossom is in the open air.

When you realize the Tao, your body will be in the sphere of the ordinary, but your mind will be in the realm of the sages. Nowadays, people want to avoid death forever and at the same time leave the ordinary world. They are very foolish, indeed, and have not even glimpsed the true principle of the Tao.

From WANG CHONGYANG: *Fifteen Articles on Establishing the Teaching* [12th century CE]; Kohn, 1993: 92

TAOIST MORAL PRINCIPLES

MORAL ADVICE

As a spiritual path, Taoism has its own set of ethical ideals and prescriptions. They follow directly from the nature of the Tao, and should be practised spontaneously, without coercion. Some Taoist texts, especially parts of the Zhuangzi, but also the Daodejing, *attack the Confucian code of ethics, which they see as artificially and externally imposed on people destroying their original or innate goodness. When society starts to praise morality, it means that morality has already been lost.*

In the following, the two sides of Taoist morality are exemplified: first the positive ideals, next the critique of corrupt morality. Among the positive Taoist virtues mentioned are modesty (humility), frugality, contentment, compassion.

WHO MAKES a show of himself, does not shine.
Who affirms himself, is not recognized.
Who shows off, has no credit.
Who brags, does not last long.

Daodejing 24

WHO KNOWS others is smart;
    who knows himself is brilliant.
Who overcomes others has physical strength,
    who overcomes himself is strong.
Who knows to have enough is rich,
    who acts with strength has determination.
Who does not lose his place lasts long,
    who dies but is not forgotten has longevity.

Daodejing 33

DIGNITY IS based on modesty.
High rank is rooted in humility.

Daodejing 39

EXCESSIVE LOVE certainly entails great waste.
Storing too much certainly results in heavy losses.
To know enough is no disgrace.
To know when to stop one avoids danger.
One is then able to last long.

Daodejing 44

WHOEVER DESIRES to be great
  does well to lower himself.

Daodejing 61

I HAVE three treasures, which I hold firm and protect.
The first one is compassionate love;
The second one is thrift;
The third one is not-daring-to-be-first in the land.
With compassionate love, one can be courageous;
With thrift, one can expand one's territory;
Not-daring-to-be-first in the land, one can
  become the leader of all able talents.

Daodejing 67

IN AN age of Perfect Virtue the worthy are not honoured, the talented are not employed. Rulers are like the high branches of a tree, the people like the deer of the fields. They do what is right but they do not know that this is righteousness. They love one another but they do not know that this is benevolence. They are truehearted but do not know that this is loyalty. They are trustworthy but do not know that this is good faith. They wriggle around like insects, performing services for one another, but do not know that they are being kind. Therefore they move without leaving any trail behind, act without leaving any memory of their deeds.

Zhuangzi 12: 'Heaven and Earth'; Watson: 138

THE PEOPLE have their constant inborn nature. To weave for their clothing, to till for their food – this is the Virtue they share.

. . . in a time of Perfect Virtue the gait of men is slow and ambling; their gaze is steady and mild. In such an age mountains have no paths or trails, lakes no boats or bridges . . .

In this age of Perfect Virtue men live the same as birds and beasts, group themselves side by side with the ten thousand things. Who then knows anything about 'gentleman' or 'petty man'? Dull and unwitting, men have no wisdom; thus their virtue does not depart from them. . . . In uncarved simplicity the people attain their true nature.

Zhuangzi 9: 'Horses' Hoofs'; Watson: 105

This spontaneous simple goodness of human nature was spoiled by the moral preaching of the Confucian 'sages'; they told the people to do what they already did naturally, thus causing doubts and divisions to arise.

I F THE Way and its Virtue had not been cast aside, how would there be any call for benevolence and righteousness? . . .

That the Way and its Virtue were destroyed in order to create benevolence and righteousness – this was the fault of the sage.

Then for the first time people learned . . . to covet knowledge, to fight to the death over profit, and there was no stopping them. This in the end was the fault of the sage.

Zhuangzi 9: 'Horses' Hoofs'; Watson: 105–6

I T IS not for the sake of reputation that you do good, but reputation follows. You expect reputation without benefit, but benefit comes. You expect benefit without contention, but contention arrives. Therefore a gentleman must be careful when he does good.

Liezi 8: 'Explaining Conjunctions'; Graham: 177

WEAKNESS IS STRENGTH

That weakness can be turned into strength is one of the paradoxes of Taoism. Tao, the Ultimate Power, works in weakness. Therefore, weakness, softness, flexibility and yielding are sources of inner strength and vitality, whereas brute force often ends in defeat. Weakness is another aspect of wuwei.

THE METHOD of Tao is weakness.

Daodejing 36

WHAT IS flexible and weak
   overcomes the hard and strong.

Daodejing 36

NOTHING UNDER heaven is softer and more flexible than water,
but in attacking the hard and rigid nothing is
more effective.

That the flexible overcomes the rigid, the soft overcomes
the hard, nobody under-heaven does not know,
but nobody can put it into practice.

Daodejing 78

WHEN ALIVE, a person is tender and flexible.
When he is dead, he is hard and rigid.
When alive, all beings and plants are tender and pliant,
When they are dead, they are dry and withered.
Indeed: the hard and rigid are companions of death.
The tender and flexible are companions of life.
Therefore, if an army is rigid it will not win victory.
If a tree is rigid, it will perish.
To be rigid and great is inferior,
to be tender and flexible is superior.

Daodejing 76

BE FLEXIBLE and you remain whole,
    be crooked and you become straight . . .
Indeed, is the old saying 'be flexible and you remain
    whole' an idle saying?
He will truly 'remain whole' and reach his destiny.

Daodejing 22

IN THE world there is a Way by which one will always conquer and there is a way by which one will never conquer. The former is called Weakness, the latter is called Strength. The two are easy to recognize, but still men do not recognize them. Hence the saying of the men of the most ancient times: 'The strong surpass those weaker than themselves, the weak surpass those stronger than themselves.'

The man who surpasses men weaker than himself is in danger when he meets someone as strong as himself, but the man who surpasses men stronger than himself is never in danger.

Liezi 2: 'The Yellow Emperor'; Graham: 52

IF YOUR aim is to be hard, you must guard it by being
  soft.
If your aim is to be strong, you must maintain it by
  being weak.
What begins soft and accumulates must become hard.
What begins weak and accumulates must become
  strong.
Watch them accumulate, and you will know where
  blessing and disaster come from.
The strong conquer those weaker than themselves,
  and when they meet an equal have no advantage.
The weak conquer those stronger than themselves,
  their force is immeasurable.

Liezi 2: 'The Yellow Emperor'; Graham: 53

NATURALNESS

One of the basic principles of Taoist philosophy is naturalness, or spontaneity. It is the pattern of action created by the Tao and, hopefully, imitated by the ten thousand beings. It relates to the theme of 'the heavenly and the human', discussed earlier. Both the Liezi and the Zhuangzi carry stories to illustrate this principle.

CONFUCIUS WAS seeing the sights at Lüliang, where the water falls from a height of thirty fathoms and races and boils along for forty *li*, so swift that no fish or other water creature can swim in it. He saw a man dive into the water and, supposing that the man was in some kind of trouble and intended to end his life, he ordered his disciples to line up on the bank and pull the man out. But after the man had gone a couple of hundred paces, he came out of the water and began strolling along the base of the embankment, his hair streaming down, singing a song. Confucius ran after him and said, 'At first I thought you were a ghost, but now I see you're a man. May I ask if you have some special way of staying afloat in the water?'

'I have no way. I began with what I was used to, grew up with my nature, and let things come to completion with fate. I go under with the swirls and come out with the eddies, following along the way the water goes and never thinking about myself. That's how I can stay afloat.'

Confucius said, 'What do you mean by saying that you began with what you were used to, grew up with your nature, and let things come to completion with fate?'

'I was born on the dry land and felt safe on the dry land – that was what I was used to. I grew up with the water and felt safe in the water – that was my nature. I don't know why I do what I do – that's fate.'

Zhuangzi 19: 'Mastering Life'; Watson: 204–5

WHEN CONFUCIUS was on his way to Chu, he passed through a forest where he saw a hunchback catching cicadas with a sticky pole as easily as though he were grabbing them with his hand.

Confucius said, 'What skill you have! Is there a special way to this?'

'I have a way,' said the hunchback. 'For the first five or six months I practise balancing two balls on top of each other on the end of the pole and, if they don't fall off, I know I will lose very few cicadas. Then I balance three balls and, if they don't fall off, I know I'll lose only one cicada in ten. Then I balance five balls and, if they don't fall off, I know it will be as easy as grabbing them with my hand. I hold my body like a stiff tree trunk and use my arm like an old dry limb. No matter how huge heaven and earth, or how numerous the ten thousand things, I'm aware of nothing but cicada wings. Not wavering, not tipping, not letting any of the other ten thousand things take the place of those cicada wings – how can I help but succeed?'

Zhuangzi 19: 'Mastering Life'; Watson: 199–200

TIMELINESS IN ACTION

As the Daodejing states in Chapter 8, timeliness, or choosing the right time is the correct standard of action. The Liezi has recorded a story of two contrasting families in which the principle of right timing is clearly manifest.

The story can be paraphrased as follows: Mr Shi had two talented sons, one loved learning, the other loved war. They went to offer their services at the courts of two states, and were welcomed by their respective kings: one to serve as tutor of his sons, the other as a strategist in charge of the army. Both received honour and high salaries.

Their neighbour, Mr Meng, also had two talented sons, trained in the same professions. When they offered their services to the rulers of other states, they were received with mistrust: one was castrated and sent back home; the other's feet were cut off to avoid his serving a rival king.

Mr Meng, greatly distressed, went to complain to his neighbour, Mr Shi, who said to him:

PICK THE right time and flourish,
Miss the right time and perish.

Your way was the same as ours, yet you failed where we succeeded – not because you did the wrong things, but because you picked the wrong time to do them. In any case, nowhere is there a principle which is right in all circumstances, or an action that is wrong in all circumstances. The method we used yesterday we may discard today and use again in the future; there are no fixed right and wrong to decide whether we use it or not.

Liezi 8: 'Explaining Conjunctions'; Graham: 162–3

ADVICE ON HEALTHFUL LIVING

The following are quotations from famous Taoist masters, mostly from the Tang dynasty (618–906) and Song dynasty (960–1279). They give advice on physical hygiene, but not separated from mental discipline. The goal of hygiene and diet is ultimately to refine body, mind and spirit to reach oneness with the Tao and, for those who aspire to it, to obtain longevity.

T HE BODY must often be exercised. Food should not be taken in excess. Do not overwork. During youth one should have enough nutrition. Avoid too greasy and sweet foods, take sweet and sour in moderation. Avoid worrying too much, don't go to extremes in happiness and anger. Avoid chasing and running around. Be moderate in sexual activity.

TAO HONGJING (456–536): *Yangsheng Yanminlu;* trans. J. Pas, from *Dictionary of Famous Quotations:* 412

I N ORDER to keep one's body healthy, one certainly must understand how to avoid these extremes: great anger, strong desires, and overindulgence in drinking and intoxication.

If one of those three occurs, one should avoid harming the true original breaths (energies) within one's body.

SUN SIMIAO (581–682): *Weisheng ge*; trans. J. Pas, from *Dictionary of Famous Quotations*: 412

D URING ONE'S lifetime, one should not allow profit and desires to disturb one's thoughts; one should not overindulge in food so as to hurt one's physical body. With a peaceful mind, in simplicity and quietness, allow one's inner balance and harmony to develop spontaneously. This way, one's seminal and spiritual essence remain firmly established within one's physical body; the original *qi* (breath, energy) preserves the essence; the mind stays in harmony with the original *qi*; one's thoughts make the mind restful; quietude makes one's thoughts peaceful and fixed.

When all this is done, one does not consciously strive to prolong one's life, yet one's life time is spontaneously lengthened.

DU GUANTING (850–933): *Daodezhenjing guang shengyi*, 36; trans. J. Pas, from *Dictionary of Famous Quotations*: 415

IF ONE'S inner mind has no thoughts nor desires, the spirit gathers and is not scattered. This is the way of preserving and nourishing life. Only if the belly has enough food, can the seminal essence be complete. Only then can one reach longevity.

LI LIN (Song dynasty): *Daodezhenjing gushanji;* trans. J. Pas; from *Dictionary of Famous Quotations*: 415–16

ONE SHOULD know that the greatest hermits live within the city. Do not search for those, who, deep in the mountains and forests, live a secluded and isolated life of self-denial. Great hermits live within the cities and transcend those who live a life of seclusion.

ZHANG BODUAN (984–1082): *Wuzhenpian;* trans. J. Pas; from *Dictionary of Famous Quotations*: 416

ONE WORKS the land for food, raises silkworms for clothing. When clothing and food are sufficient, then all the wealth under heaven becomes superfluous. It's like when one is thirsty and drinks from the river; once one has drunk enough, one no longer admires the great flow.

JI KANG (Three Kingdoms Period): *Da xiangzi qinan yangshenglun;* trans. J. Pas, from *Dictionary of Famous Quotations*: 417

The mind is a formidable tool that should not be meddled with.

CUI ZHU was questioning Lao Dan [Laozi]. 'If you do not govern the world, then how can you improve men's minds?'

Lao Dan said: 'Be careful – don't meddle with men's minds! Men's minds can be forced down or boosted up, but this downing and upping imprisons and brings death to the mind. Gentle and shy, the mind can bend the hard and the strong; it can chisel and cut away, carve and polish. Its heat is that of burning fire, its coldness that of solid ice, its swiftness such that, in the time it takes to lift and lower the head, it has twice swept over the four seas and beyond. At rest, it is deep-fathomed and still; in movement, it is far-flung as the heavens, racing and galloping out of reach of all bounds. This indeed is the mind of man!'

Zhuangzi 11: 'Let it Be, Leave it Alone'; Watson: 116

THE MIND of man is more perilous than mountains or rivers, harder to understand than Heaven. Heaven at least has its fixed times of spring and fall, winter and summer, daybreak and dusk. But man is thick-skinned and hides his true form deep within.

Zhuangzi 32: 'Lie Yukou'; Watson: 358

LANGUAGE, DREAMS AND UTOPIAS

THE USE OF THE USELESS

A paradoxical Taoist theme, especially found in the Zhuangzi, is the use of the useless. Trees whose wood is worthless, or that produce no fruit, have the best chance of living a long life: nobody will bother them or hack them down. Applied to human beings, it is better to be useless (in a political sense) than to be talented. Otherwise one would expect a government appointment with all its potential dangers and uncertainties.

ZHUANGZI WAS walking in the mountains when he saw a huge tree, its branches and leaves thick and lush. A woodcutter paused by its side but made no move to cut it down. When Zhuangzi asked the reason, he replied: 'There's nothing it could be used for!' Zhuangzi said, 'Because of its worthlessness, this tree is able to live out the years Heaven gave it.'

Zhuangzi 20: 'The Mountain Tree'; Watson: 209

IN SONG [there is a region that] is fine for growing catalpas, cypresses and mulberries. But those that are more than one or two arm-lengths around are cut down for people who want monkey perches; those that are three or four spans around are cut down for the ridgepoles of tall roofs, and those that are seven or eight spans are cut down for the families of nobles or rich merchants who want side boards for coffins. So they never get to live out the years Heaven gave them, but are cut down in mid-journey by axes. This is the danger of being usable.

Zhuangzi 4: 'In the World of Men'; Watson: 65

HUIZI SAID to Zhuangzi: 'I have a big tree of the kind men call *shu*. Its trunk is too gnarled and bumpy to apply a measuring line to, its branches too bent and twisty to match up a compass or square. You could stand it by the road and no carpenter would look at it twice. Your words, too, are big and useless, and so everyone alike spurns them!'

Zhuangzi said: 'Maybe you've never seen a wildcat or a weasel. It crouches down and hides, watching for something to come along. It leaps and races east and west, not hesitating to go high or low – until it falls into the trap and dies in the net. . . .

'Now you have this big tree and you're distressed because it's useless. Why don't you plant it in Not-Even-Anything Village, or the field of Broad-and Boundless, relax and do nothing by its side, or lie down for a free and easy sleep under it? Axes will never shorten its life, nothing can ever harm it. If there is no use for it, how can it come to grief or pain?'

Zhuangzi 1: 'Free Flight into Transcendence'; Watson: 35

HUIZI SAID to Zhuangzi: 'Your words are useless!' Zhuangzi said: 'A man has to understand the useless before you can talk to him about the useful. The earth is certainly vast and broad, though a man uses no more of it than the area he puts his feet on. If, however, you were to dig away all the earth around his feet until you reached the Yellow Springs [the Chinese Underworld], then would the man still be able to make use of it?'

'No, it would be useless,' said Huizi.

'It is obvious, then,' said Zhuangzi, 'that the useless has its use.'

Zhuangzi 26: 'External Things'; Watson: 299

Being in poor physical shape, one gets looked after! Being without talents or having 'crippled virtue', one avoids government service and may live a long life!

THERE'S CRIPPLED Shu: chin stuck down in his navel, shoulders up above his head, pigtail pointing at the sky, his five organs on top, his two thighs pressing his ribs. By sewing and washing, he gets enough to fill his mouth; by handling a winnow and sorting out the good grain, he makes enough to feed ten people. When the authorities call out the troops, he stands in the crowd waving goodbye; when they get up a big work party, they pass him over because he's a chronic invalid. And when they are doling out grain to the ailing, he gets three big measures and ten bundles of firewood. With a crippled body, he's still able to look after himself and finish out the years Heaven gave him. How much better, then, if he had crippled virtue!

Zhuangzi 4: 'In the World of Men'; Watson: 66

ZIQI OF Nanbo was wandering around the Hill of Shang when he saw a huge tree there, different from all the rest. A thousand teams of horses could have taken shelter under it and its shade would have covered them all. Ziqi said, 'What tree is this? It must certainly have some extraordinary usefulness!' But, looking up, he saw that the smaller limbs were gnarled and twisted, unfit for beams or rafters, and looking down, he saw that the trunk was pitted and rotten and could not be used for coffins. He licked one of the leaves and it blistered his mouth and made it sore. He sniffed the odour and it was enough to make a man drunk for three days. 'It turns out to be a completely unusable tree,' said Ziqi, 'and so it has been able to grow up this big. Aha! – it is this unusableness that the Holy Man makes use of!'

Zhuangzi 4: 'In the World of Men'; Watson: 65

DREAMS AND THE LIMITATIONS OF
LANGUAGE AND KNOWLEDGE

Words are unable to express the inexpressible. Words are finite: the Real is infinite. Words are useful as tools for understanding; once one has understood, words should be dismissed. The Tao is inexpressible through language; words about the Tao are just scratches on the surface of reality.

THE FISH trap exists because of the fish; once you've got the fish, you can forget the trap. The rabbit snare exists because of the rabbit; once you've got the rabbit, you can forget the snare. Words exist because of meaning; once you've got the meaning, you can forget the words. Where can I find a man who has forgotten words so I can have a word with him?

Zhuangzi 26: 'External Things'; Watson: 302

TAO EXPRESSIBLE in words is not the everlasting Tao. Names which are nameable are not everlasting names.

Daodejing 1

Chapter 2 of the Zhuangzi presents a deep reflection on the nature of language. As a tool for communication, language has its uses. Yet, very often it is abused and obscures the nature of reality. Language is not an absolute! Neither is knowledge an absolute. When we believe we know things, perhaps we do not know them at all. When we think we are awake and conscious, perhaps we live in a dream. What is the difference between what we perceive of as consciousness and the state of dreaming? Zhuangzi enjoys discussing dream versus reality and so does Liezi, who has an entire chapter devoted to it.

WORDS ARE not just wind. Words have something to say. But if what they have to say is not fixed, then do they really say something? Or do they say nothing? People suppose that words are different from the peeps of baby birds, but is there any difference, or isn't there?

How is it that the Way is obscured to the point that there is 'real' and 'unreal'? How is it that language is obscured to the point that there is affirmation and negation?

The Way is obscured by small achievements; language is obscured by vain eloquence.

Zhuangzi 2: 'The Identification of Things and Theories';
Watson: 39, with some modifications

NIE QUE asked Wang Ni, 'Do you know what all things agree in calling right?'

'How would I know that?' said Wang Ni.

'Do you know that you don't know it?'

'How would I know that?'

'Then do things know nothing?'

'How would I know that? However, suppose I try saying something. What way do I have of knowing that if I say I know something I don't really know it? Or what way do I have of knowing that if I say I don't know something I don't really in fact know it?'

Zhuangzi 2: 'The Identification of Things and Theories';
Watson: 45

How do we know the difference between dream and reality? Is there a difference? Or are the two so intermixed that there is no way of distinguishing them? The problem is dramatized in the famous story of Zhuangzi's butterfly dream. The answer remains uncertain: there are no convincing criteria to decide one way or another:

How do I know that loving life is not a delusion? How do I know that in hating death I am not like a man who having left home in his youth, has forgotten the way back? . . . How do I know that the dead do not wonder why they ever longed for life?

He who dreams of drinking wine may weep when morning comes; he who dreams of weeping may in the morning go off to hunt. While he is dreaming he does not know it is a dream, and in his dream he may even try to interpret a dream. Only after he wakes does he know it was a dream. And someday there will be a great awakening when we know that this is all a great dream.

Zhuangzi 2: 'The Identification of Things and Theories';
Watson: 47

Once Zhuang Zhou (Zhuangzi) dreamt he was a butterfly flitting and fluttering around, happy with himself, and doing as he pleased. He didn't know he was Zhuang Zhou. Suddenly he woke up and there he was, solid and unmistakable Zhuang Zhou. But he didn't know if he was Zhuang Zhou who had dreamt he was a butterfly, or a butterfly dreaming he was Zhuang Zhou. Between Zhuang Zhou and a butterfly there must be some distinction!

Zhuangzi 2: 'The Identification of Things and Theories';
Watson: 49

Is it possible that for some people a dream is more real and more comforting than real life? The following Liezi story seems to imply this.

M R YIN of Zhou ran a huge estate. The underlings who hurried to serve him never rested from dawn to dusk. There was an old servant with no more strength in his muscles, whom he drove all the harder. By day the servant went to work groaning, at night he slept soundly dulled by fatigue. Losing consciousness, every evening he dreamed that he was lord of the state, enthroned above the people, with all affairs of state under his control. He gave himself up to whatever pleased him, excursions and banquets, palaces and spectacles; his joy was incomparable. Waking, he was a servant again.

When someone condoled with him for having to work so hard, the servant said:

'Man's term of life is a hundred years, divided between day and night. By day I am a bondman, and my life is bitter indeed; but at night I become a prince, and my joy is incomparable. Why should I complain?'

Liezi 3: 'King Mu of Zhou'; Graham: 68

Another enigmatic story is found in the Liezi. It seems to say that individual identity is an illusion, that our short lives, once over, are as if they never happened.

WHEN LIEZI was eating at the roadside on a journey to Wei, he saw a skull a hundred years old. He picked a stalk, pointed at it, and said, turning to his disciple: 'Only he and I know that you were never born and will never die. Is it he who is truly miserable, is it we who are truly happy?'

Liezi 1: 'Heaven's Gifts'; Graham: 20–1

UTOPIAN IDEALS

Descriptions of utopian paradises or states of 'primitive' happiness are found in many traditions. The Taoists, too, have their own versions. One is found in the Daodejing *and is often quoted – also often misunderstood – as the standard model of society. It is, in fact, the view of a minority among Taoist masters, the so-called 'primitivists', also encountered in the* Zhuangzi.

The Liezi *describes such an ideal land, situated far to the north of China, where people live in a paradise-like perfect environment.*

I T IS a place which you cannot reach by boat or carriage or on foot, only by a journey of the spirit. In this country there are no teachers and leaders; all things follow their natural course. The people have no cravings and lusts; all men follow their natural course. They are incapable of delighting in life or hating death, and therefore prefer themselves to others, and so they neither love nor hate. They do not know how to turn their faces to things or turn their backs, go with the stream or push against it, so nothing benefits or harms them. There is nothing at all which they grudge or regret, nothing which they dread or envy. They go into water without drowning, into fire without burning; hack them, flog them, there is no wound nor pain; poke them, scratch them, there is no ache nor itch. They ride space as though walking the solid earth, sleep on the void as though on their beds; clouds and mist do not hinder their sight, thunder does not confuse their hearing, beauty and ugliness do not disturb their hearts, mountains and valleys do not trip their feet – for they make only journeys of the spirit.

Liezi 2: 'The Yellow Emperor'; Graham: 34

[THINK OF] a small state with a low population.
Let there be tens or hundreds of tools, they are not
    used.
Let the people be serious about death, they do not
    travel far.
Though there are boats and carriages, there is no one
    who rides in them.
Though there are armour and weapons, there is no
    one to display them.
Let people knot strings again and use them [for
    counting].

They savour their food, beautify their clothing, enjoy
  their dwelling, are happy with their customs.
Although neighbouring states can look at each other,
  and roosters and dogs can be mutually heard,
The people grow old and die, without visiting each
  other.

Daodejing 80

In ancient times, before the Way was darkened by human interference, men and animals lived peacefully together. There is, in fact, no essential difference between humans and animals.

THERE ARE ways in which the intelligence of beasts and birds is by nature similar to man's. They wish as much as we do to preserve their lives, and do not have to borrow from man's wisdom to do so. Buck and doe mate together, mother and child keep close together; they shun the plains and choose inaccessible places, avoid cold and seek out warmth; they live in herds and travel in formations with the young ones on the inside and the fully grown on the outside; they lead each other to water and call to each other when they find food.

In the most ancient times men and animals lived together and walked side by side. In the time of the Five Emperors and the Three Kings [according to the Taoists the beginning of decay], the animals were frightened away and scattered for the first time. In our own degenerate times, they crouch in hiding and flee to their lairs to avoid harm.

Liezi 2: 'The Yellow Emperor'; Graham: 54–5

In Buddhism and Hinduism, humans and animals are all called 'sentient beings', which means they are capable of feeling and perception, and are conscious. Many stories and legends depict this closeness. Buddhists perform seasonal rites to save animals from their lower status and preach to them; even the Christian Saint Francis once addressed the birds and fishes. The ancient Taoist sages also realized the essential oneness of all species.

EVEN NOW in the country of Jie in the East, there are many people who understand the speech of domestic animals; this is a discovery possible even to our own limited knowledge. The divine sages of the most ancient times knew the habits of all the myriad things, and interpreted the cries of all the different species; they called them together for meetings and gave them instructions, as though they were human beings. So the fact that the sages would meet the spirits and goblins first, next summon the human beings of the eight quarters and finally assemble the birds and beasts and insects, implies that there are no great differences in mind and intelligence between living species. The divine sages knew that this was the case, and therefore in teaching they left out none of them.

Liezi 2: 'The Yellow Emperor'; Graham: 55

It is a common Buddhist practice in China to release animals from their captivity. It is considered an act of compassion and earns great merit. The Liezi, too, refers to this custom, perhaps influenced by Buddhism. But, after all, this is viewed by Taoists as a misguided practice, and as such the following story suggests a critique of Buddhism.

THE PEOPLE of Handan presented doves to [their lord] on New Year's morning. When a visitor asked the reason, [the lord] explained: 'We release living things on New Year's Day as a gesture of kindness.'

'The people know you wish to release them, so they vie with each other to catch them, and many of the doves die. If you wish to keep them alive, it would be better to forbid the people to catch them. When you release doves after catching them, the kindness does not make up for the mistake.'

'You are right,' said [the lord].

Liezi 8: 'Explaining Conjunctions'; Graham: 178

AMUSING STORIES

The following are rather anecdotes – amusing, but also showing a deep understanding of the human mind and a calm irony towards sages and political leaders.

THERE WAS a man who lost his axe, and suspected the boy next door. He watched the boy walking: he had stolen the axe! His expression, his talk, his behaviour, his manner, everything about him betrayed that he had stolen the axe.

Soon afterwards the man was digging in his garden and found the axe. On another day he saw the boy next door again: nothing in his behaviour and manner suggested that he would steal an axe.

Liezi 8: 'Explaining Conjunctions'; Graham: 180

WHEN CONFUCIUS was travelling in the East, he saw two small children arguing and asked them the reason. One child said he thought that the sun is nearer to us at sunrise, the other that it is nearer at noon. The first child said:

'When the sun first rises it is as big as the cover of a car; by noon it is as small as a plate or a bowl. Don't you think it must be nearer when it is big than when it is small?'

The other child answered: 'When the sun first rises the air is cool, by noon it is like dipping your hand in hot water. Don't you think it must be nearer when it is hot than when it is cool?'

Confucius could not decide the question. The two children laughed: 'Who says you are a learned man?'

Liezi 5: 'The Questions of Tang'; Graham; 104–5

WHEN HUIZI was prime minister of Liang, Zhuangzi set off to visit him. Someone said to Huizi, 'Zhuangzi is coming because he wants to replace you as prime minister!' With this, Huizi was filled with alarm and searched all over the state for three days and three nights trying to find Zhuangzi. Zhuangzi then came to see him and said, 'In the south there is a bird called the Yuanchu – I wonder if you've ever heard of it? The Yuanchu rises up from the South Sea and flies to the North Sea, and it will rest on nothing but the Wutong tree, eat nothing but the fruit of the Lian, and drink only from springs of sweet water. Once there was an owl who had got hold of a half-rotten old rat, and as the Yuanchu passed by, it raised its head, looked up at the Yuanchu, and said, "Shoo!" Now that you have this Liang state of yours, are you trying to shoo me?'

Zhuangzi 17: 'Autumn Floods'; Watson: 188

ZHUANGZI AND Huizi were strolling along the dam of the Hao River when Zhuangzi said, 'See how the minnows come out and dart around where they please! That's what fish really enjoy!'

Huizi said, 'You're not a fish – how do you know what fish enjoy?'

Zhuangzi said, 'You're not I, so how do you know I don't know what fish enjoy?'

Huizi said, 'I'm not you, so I certainly don't know what you know. On the other hand, you're certainly not a fish – so that still proves you don't know what fish enjoy!'

Zhuangzi said, 'Let's go back to your original question, please. You asked me how I know what fish enjoy – so you already knew I knew it when you asked the question. I know it by standing here beside the Hao.'

Zhuangzi 17: 'Autumn Floods'; Watson: 188–9

ONCE, WHEN Zhuangzi was fishing in the Pu River, the king of Chu sent two officials to go and announce to him: 'I would like to trouble you with the administration of my realm.'

Zhuangzi held on to the fishing pole, and without turning his head, said, 'I have heard that there is a sacred tortoise in Chu that has been dead for three thousand years. The king keeps it wrapped in cloth and boxed, and stores it in the ancestral temple. Now would this tortoise rather be dead and have its bones left behind and honoured? Or would it rather be alive and dragging its tail in the mud?'

'It would rather be alive and dragging its tail in the mud,' said the two officials.

Zhuangzi said, 'Go away! I'll drag my tail in the mud!'

Zhuangzi 17: 'Autumn Floods'; Watson: 187–8

AMAZING STORY

If we recall that the Liezi *was edited in the third century* CE, *but contains much older material, it comes as a great surprise to find in it a story of medical practice that predates medical history by 2000 years. The* Liezi *narrates the story of a heart transplant that is both fantastic and unbelievable. It is based on the Chinese conception that 'mental functions are located in the heart instead of the brain' (Graham: 107). Here is the story with some minor changes.*

MR HU and Mr Ying fell ill, and both asked Dr Pian to treat them. Pian did treat them and when they had both recovered told them:

'You have just been suffering from diseases which attacked your organs from outside, and which of course medicine and the needle can cure. But you also have diseases which were born with you and have grown with the growth of your bodies; would you like me to treat them for you?'

'First tell us what makes you think so?'

'Your ambition is greater than your energy,' said Pian to Mr Hu. 'So that you are capable of forming plans but seldom come to decisions. Mr Ying's energy is greater than his ambition, so that he rarely thinks ahead and comes to grief by acting irresponsibly. If I exchange your hearts you will benefit by the equalizing of ambition and energy.'

[The two patients agreed.]

Then Dr Pian gave the two men drugged wine, and they lost consciousness for three days. He cut open their breasts, pulled out their hearts, exchanged them, put them back, and applied a magic medicine. When they woke up they were as well as before.

The two men took their leave and went off home. Thereupon Mr Hu returned to Mr Yang's house and took possession of his wife and children, who did not recognize him. Mr Ying likewise returned to Mr Hu's house and took possession of his wife and children, who also did not recognize him. So the two families went to law against each other, and called on Dr Pian to explain. Dr Pian explained the cause, and the litigants were satisfied.

Liezi 5: 'The Questions of Tang'; Graham: 106–7

PARADOXES

Characteristic of Taoist writing, and especially of the Daodejing, is the use of paradox. It is perhaps a strategy designed to shock and bring home some truths, vigorously and convincingly, that normal language could never achieve. Paradoxes are possibly the forerunners of the famous koan (gongan) *method used by the Chinese Chan (Zen) masters to 'shock' the mind into awakening.*

In previous sections a great number of paradoxes have already been quoted, such as for example under wuwei: *to pursue learning is to increase every day; to pursue the Tao one has to decrease every day.* (Daodejing 48).

BE EMPTY and you are filled
    be worn out and you are renewed.
Possess little and you become rich.
    possess much and you are tormented.

Daodejing 22

SUPERIOR POWER (virtue) is not power.
   therefore it has power.
Inferior power (virtue) does not abandon its power,
   therefore it has no power.

Daodejing 38

GREAT PERFECTION seems defective
   [but] in its operations it is not exhausted.
Great fullness seems empty,
   [but] in its operations it is not depleted.
Great straightness seems crooked.
Great skill seems clumsy.
Great eloquence seems to stutter.

Daodejing 45

WITHOUT GOING out of the door
   one [is able to] know the world [under-heaven].
Without looking out of the window
   one [is able to] observe the way of heaven.
The further one goes away
   the less one knows.

Daodejing 47

AS SOON as one is born, one enters death.

Daodejing 50

TO PERCEIVE the small is called insight.
To hold on to weakness is called strength.

Daodejing 52

WHO KNOWS does not speak.
Who speaks does not know.

Daodejing 56

WHO PROMISES too lightly, certainly lacks
    trustworthiness.
Who thinks things are easy, certainly hits many
    difficulties.
Therefore, the sage regards things as difficult.
And thus never encounters difficulties.

Daodejing 63

A TREE that fills many arms' embrace,
    grows from a tiny twig.
A tower of nine stories high
    rises from a pile of dirt.
A thousand *li* journey
    starts below one's feet.

Daodejing 64

MY WORDS are very easy to understand and very easy to
    practise,
Yet nobody under-heaven can understand them or can
    practise them.

Daodejing 70

TO KNOW that one does not know is superior.
Not to know [but to claim] to know is sickness.

Daodejing 71

TRUE WORDS sound like their opposite.

Daodejing 78

TRUTHFUL WORDS are not pleasing,
Pleasing words are not truthful.
Good people do not argue.
Those who argue are not good.
Those who know have no erudition.
Those who have erudition do not know.

Daodejing 81

I T IS easy to keep from walking; the hard thing is to walk without touching the ground. It is easy to cheat when you work for men, but hard to cheat when you work for Heaven. You have heard of flying with wings, but you have never heard of flying without wings. You have heard of the knowledge that knows, but you have never heard of the knowledge that does not know. Look into that closed room, the empty chamber where brightness is born! Fortune and blessing gather where there is stillness.

Zhuangzi 4: 'In the World of Men'; Watson: 58

REFERENCES

Ames, R. 1983. *The Art of Rulership. A Study in Ancient Chinese Political Thought*. Honolulu, University of Hawaii Press.

Chen, Qifu, editor-in-chief. 1994. *Ru-Dao-Fo Mingyan Cidian* [*Dictionary of Famous Quotations from Confucianism, Taoism and Buddhism*]. Zhengzhou (Henan), People's Publishing Co. of Henan, China.

Graham, A.C., trans. 1960. *The Book of Lieh-tzu*, 2nd edn. New York, Grove Press.

Kohn, L. 1987a. *Seven Steps to the Tao: Sima Chengzhen's Zuowanglun*. Monumenta Serica Monograph Series, Vol. 20. Nettetal (Germany): Steyler Verlag.

Kohn, L. 1987b. 'The Teaching of Tianyinzi'. *Journal of Chinese Religions*, 15, 1–28.

Kohn, L., ed. 1993. *The Taoist Experience*. Albany, NY, SUNY Press.

Lopez, D., ed. 1996. *Religions of China in Practice*. Princeton, Princeton University Press.

Major, J. 1993. *Heaven and Earth in Early Han Thought. Chapters Three, Four and Five of the Huananzi*. Albany, NY, SUNY Press.

Needham, J. 1956. Science and Civilization in China (Vol. 2). Cambridge, Cambridge University Press.

Pas, J., trans. 1997. *The Tao Te Ching*. Unpublished translation.

Robinet, I. 1993. *Taoist Meditation*. trans. J. Pas and N. Girardot. Albany, NY, SUNY Press.

Watson, B., trans. 1970. *The Complete Works of Chuang Tzu*. New York and London, Columbia University Press.

妙